Epworth Commentaries

General Editor
Ivor H. Jones

The Epistles to the Thessalonians

The Epistles to
THE THESSALONIANS

IVOR H. JONES

✠ EPWORTH

British Library Cataloguing in Publication data

A catalogue record for this book is available
from the British Library

0-7162-0595-5

First published in 2005
by Epworth Press
4 John Wesley Road
Werrington
Peterborough PE4 6ZP

Printed and bound in Great Britain by
William Clowes Ltd, Beccles, Suffolk

CONTENTS

Contents

GENERAL INTRODUCTION

The *Epworth Preacher's Commentaries* that Greville P. Lewis edited in the 1950s and 1960s having served their turn, the Epworth Press commissioned a team of distinguished academics who are also preachers and teachers to create a new series of commentaries to serve readers into the twenty-first century. We took the opportunity offered by the publication in 1989 of the Revised English Bible to use this very readable and scholarly version as the basis of our commentaries, and are grateful to the Oxford and Cambridge University Presses for the requisite licences.

Just as the books that make up the Bible differ in their provenance and purpose, so our authors have necessarily differed in the structure and bearing of their commentaries. But they have attempted to get as close as possible to the intention of the original writers, expounding their texts in the light of the place, time, circumstances, and culture that gave them birth, showing why each work was received by Jews and Christians into their respective Canons of Holy Scripture. They have sought also to make full use of the dramatic advances in biblical scholarship world-wide but at the same time to explain technical terms in the language of the common reader, and to suggest ways in which Scripture can help towards the living of the Christian life today. They have endeavoured to produce commentaries that can be used with confidence in ecumenical, multiracial, and multifaith situations, and not by scholars only but by preachers, teachers, students, church members, and anyone who wishes to improve his or her understanding of the Bible.

This series has now come to an end, and it is my pleasure in this last of the series to thank all who have contributed volumes and all who have assisted in the process of their publication.

Ivor H. Jones

PREFACE

The work on the Epworth Commentaries has owed a great debt to the members of the Editorial Committee and to those who have acted as its secretaries. The first volume was published in 1990, a typically creative approach to the book of Job by Cyril Rodd. He was invited to contribute to the series by John Stacey (whose brother David, it has to be said, took especial interest in the wording of the General Introduction to the series, as well as later contributing his Isaiah 1—39 commentary). Later Cyril Rodd himself took over the secretaryship from John. Harold Guite shared the editorial responsibilities with me initially with his delightful and experienced mixture of patient professionalism and spirituality. It was during the period while Gerald Burt held that office that the arrangements for the volume on the Thessalonian correspondence had to be changed and the committee invited me to take over the commission. I should like to dedicate this volume to Gerald. He was a dear friend whom I respected greatly for the many services which he rendered Methodism, not least in his work for the Epworth Press. And now the last volume is published under the expert direction of Gerald's successor, Natalie Watson, to whom I am greatly indebted for her patience and assistance.

Within the bibliography the reader will find a recent volume entitled *Not in the Word Alone*. It records the work of the Sixteenth Ecumenical Pauline Colloquium on 1 Thessalonians which took place in the Benedictine Abbey of St Paul outside the Walls at the invitation of the Abbot, the Revd Paolo Lunardon OSB, and with Professor Morna Hooker-Stacey as its impartial chairman. It concluded with the professors who represented Thessalonica reading aloud for us the Greek of 'their' letter from Paul, a reminder that this would be how the original Thessalonian Christians met together to hear it. My indebtedness to the Colloquium, and not least to its chairman whose own work on 1 Thessalonians has been so internationally influential, will be evident at many points. For the rest of the bibliography I must pay my gratitude to the libraries that have continued to assist my research, particularly several in both Cambridge and Heidelberg. I want also to make a special mention of the seminar which Dr Nicholl led in the Cambridge Divinity Faculty and to express particular appreciation of the Appendix to his book. Over several years I had formed my own view of the difficult passage in 2 Thessalonians 2.3–8, but after working with Dr Nicholl's Appendix on 'Michael the Restrainer' I came eventually to the conclusion that probably he had broken the code. I very happily pay tribute to that particular piece of invaluable research.

Since 'kinship' terms play an important role in the Thessalonian correspondence, the uses of the word 'brother' present some problems to the maintaining of inclusive language. The distinguished history in religious circles played by the term 'friends' commends its use here in place of 'brothers'. The alternative of 'brothers/sisters' besides being clumsy would also have been at points inappropriate.

I want especially to express my appreciation for the work of Mary Matthews, the Editorial Manager, to Gill Wallis for her work on the script and to Linda Foster for her work on the proofs.

With this volume the series is complete, a fascinating conclusion in that it represents a commentary on probably the earliest extant document from the Christian tradition. The end is truly the beginning!

Ivor H. Jones
Holy Week
2005

ABBREVIATIONS

AV	Authorized Version, also known as the King James Version
BCE	Before the Common Era
CE	Common Era
GNB	Good News Bible, also known as Today's English Version
JB	Jerusalem Bible
JSOT	*Journal for the Study of the Old Testament*
LXX	Septuagint (a Greek translation of the Hebrew Bible)
MT	Masoretic Text (the received text of the Hebrew Bible)
NAB	New American Bible
NEB	New English Bible
NIV	New International Version
NJB	New Jerusalem Bible
NRSV	New Revised Standard Version
REB	Revised English Bible
RSV	Revised Standard Version
VT	*Vetus Testamentum*

INTRODUCTION

1. *The purpose of the Commentaries*

The General Introduction to this Commentary Series sets out two goals: to strive to get as close as possible to the intention of the original writer, and to contribute towards the living of the Christian life today within today's ecumenical, multiracial and multifaith situation. Since the series began in 1990 many things have changed. As far as concerns the exposition of a biblical text against its original place, time, circumstances and culture, the arguments have in some ways been strengthened, although at the time when the series began some doubted its value. An increasingly powerful case has been built for a text to be recognized as a given, and as a given with an origin, a purpose and a primary context. The technical means relevant to the exposition of a text in its original setting may have become more complex and numerous. We shall find evidence for this in the rhetorical and epistolary study of the Thessalonian correspondence. This widening technical range of scholarship, carefully used, has if anything increased the interest in and importance of the 'historical critical' method. In the case of First Thessalonians various textual factors underline that development: the likelihood that the text was initiated by the apostle Paul, that it may well be the first Christian document now extant and available to us, and the circumstances of its composition, which can be given a securer absolute dating than any other of the New Testament documents (that is to say, none of the others can be allocated to a reasonably precise year of origin).

As for the second goal, that of providing an exposition of Scripture which can contribute to contemporary Christian living, that has in many ways become more difficult during the intervening years. The more we understand of theology and ethics within first-century Christian culture the further we seem to move away from the extraordinary demands which are now daily thrust upon us. Nevertheless, we shall find that the links are there. In particular, as we look ever more closely at the text of the Thessalonian letters, we find ourselves constantly addressing some vital contemporary issues.

There is first a very practical concern. A vital issue in today's world is the need to change – that is true if the world is to survive; yet the process of change is itself so fundamental that it can often result in a damaging disorientation. The keenest observer of this process in recent years has been Iris Murdoch (Conradi, pp. 90–1). Aware that we do not live in a world where we can write the terms of our own moral reference, since demands come from beyond us which require our attention, Iris Murdoch drew from Simone Weil two significant insights. First, morality is an almost impossible counter-gravitational striving against sinfulness, a sinfulness which is so natural and irresistible it is comparable with gravity itself. Second, the attempt to change, or the experience of being changed, can be so violent a deracination that it can corrupt or demoralize. It is true that Iris Murdoch's novels which, like *The Black Prince*, examine those two features of human existence most closely, do so on the basis of a perception of human relationships as having a complexity almost beyond disentanglement. It is, however, a perception worth noting in our own questioning concerning the need for change and the practical consequences of change.

Those contemporary reflections have a precise relevance to the study of the Thessalonian correspondence. The relevance becomes evident when we find, on the one hand, Paul wrestling as a convert to Christianity himself with Jewish roots from which he could never entirely be free, and, on the other hand, those to whom he writes, whether formerly Jew or Gentile, wrestling with changes of commitment with incalculable consequences for their continued life in Thessalonica. The Thessalonian letters offer no simple solace or solution here. What they do offer, both as we attempt to understand the original intention of the text, and as we relate the text to our own circumstances, is a deepening awareness that change is beyond our faculties as individuals if what is required of us is not to be destructive. Community resources are essential, and, beyond those, a fresh understanding of what constitutes wholesome community relationships.

Alongside that practical question is a raft of theoretical questions which give special relevance to our reading of the Thessalonian letters. I name the four central ones: the place of humanity in a universe governed by the laws of thermodynamics; the future of a world buzzing with all its great religions and cultures; the purpose of the great economies of the world with their potential for peace and war; and the meaning of everyday relationships, political, social, community and family, as our knowledge of the make-up of our humanity grows.

Those four great questions cannot ultimately be answered apart from the central insight of Christianity's oldest extant documents, the Thessalonian letters. What is the insight? The nature of God's grace: God's faithfulness, trustful love and recreating power (White, pp. 17–43). It was this insight which enabled Paul, within the limits of geography and time as he knew them, to understand how in Jesus Christ God could begin to unpick the chaotic pattern of the threads woven into our existence, so as to prepare a richer life beyond the boundaries of empire, nationalism, race, social difference and death (Wainwright, pp. 274–92), and point to the self-giving style of relationships which makes that possible (Williams, pp. 225–64). The point of reading through the Thessalonian letters is to discover how for Paul, in terms of the world and realities as he understood them, God's grace could be all-transforming, making change possible without it being destructive and isolating. To discover that is to begin to look afresh at the four great questions of our modern existence.

2. *The date and circumstances for the writing of* 1 *Thessalonians*

Paul entered Europe via the ribbon road stretching from the Black Sea to Dyrrhachium on the Adriatic coast: the Via Egnatia. This took him along the key trade and troop route from the East towards Rome, by means of which Paul had access to Philippi and Thessalonica, cities with their distinctive cultures, organizations and honoured traditions, and their popular religious cults, including those of Rome and the Roman Emperor. His stay in Thessalonica was relatively brief; it was cut short by a local disturbance which forced Paul and Silvanus to flee from the city to Beroea, leaving behind a fledgling community which he could only contact via travellers, intermediaries and his colleague Timothy. Paul moved on from Beroea to Athens; and the Acts of the Apostles recounts his continued journey via Athens to Corinth.

The arrival in Corinth is an important moment from many points of view, and, among other things, for the dating of Paul's career. One of the only few examples of absolute dating within Paul's career is provided by an inscription found at Delphi, which places Gallio's proconsulship in Corinth in relation to the acclamation of Claudius as Emperor. On the basis of this evidence it is likely that Gallio was in office in Corinth from late spring or early summer of 51 CE until roughly the same time in the following year. According to Acts 18.12–17, while he was in Corinth, Paul was brought before Gallio, who ruled against his prosecutors. So Paul was probably in Corinth at some point during spring 51 CE and summer 52 CE. Gallio was brother to the philosopher and writer Seneca, to whose letters we shall later refer.

We do not know at what point during Gallio's proconsulship or at what point during Paul's stay in Corinth the hearing took place. Our only evidence on these questions is from the Acts of the Apostles, and all that Acts implies is that when the hearing took place Paul may already have been in Corinth eighteen months. Perhaps the hearing was a way of trying out the proconsul early in his tenure, in which case it would have taken place in late summer 51 CE. Paul would then have arrived in Corinth in the early spring of 50.

Although 1 Thessalonians does not actually refer to Paul's arrival in Corinth we have in 1 Thess. 3.1–10 Paul's own account of the events relating to the visit of Timothy to Thessalonica and his return back to report to Paul. Paul's response to that return, and to the good news which Timothy brought, is expressed in a thanksgiving which implies that Silvanus had joined them too (see the plural, 'We always give thanks for you all', 1 Thess. 1.2). Putting that evidence alongside what Acts relates (Acts 17.10—18.5), we can assume that all three, Paul, Silvanus and Timothy, were at that point together again, and that they were together in Corinth. Additionally, the evidence of 1 Thessalonians and Acts would make that moment the opportunity for Paul to write 1 Thessalonians, nearly half a year after they had fled from Thessalonica to Beroea. Summer to autumn 51 CE is by those calculations a possible date for 1 Thessalonians, and the circumstances for the writing of 1 Thessalonians included a part of his work in Corinth.

3. 1 Thessalonians, the first extant Christian letter

1 Thessalonians is the first extant Christian letter and the first extant letter of Paul, although he may well have written earlier ones of which we have no record. The dating of the letter, which we have just considered, suggests that it is the earliest of the Pauline letters, and there are other features which confirm its early appearance. It is one of the few Pauline letters without information in it about a charitable collection for Jerusalem, a collection on which Paul corresponded after 51 CE with several churches (1 Cor. 16.1–4; Wedderburn, pp. 95–110). His silence on the matter in 1 Thessalonians is all the more significant because eventually the collection was accompanied on its journey to Jerusalem by Aristarchus and Secundus as Thessalonian representatives (Acts 20.4; see Barrett, p. 948; Alexander, p. 1053).

It used to be claimed that 1 Thessalonians must be an early letter of Paul because of its 'eschatology' (its teaching about the Last Days). Paul's teaching on that subject had been used as a basis for trying to establish a chronological order for the Pauline letters. That approach is now questioned; Paul's letters represent primarily his pastoral responses to differing situations. The subject of the Last Days was included only when it was relevant to pastoral needs; we shall see that to be the case for 1 Thessalonians.

4. The originality of 1 Thessalonians

1 Thessalonians was the first extant Christian letter. So what guided Paul's composition of the letter? Today, if a letter is reasonably formal, we expect it to correspond with an accepted structure and layout. The same could be said of an ancient letter also. 2 Maccabees, one of the books in the REB Apocrypha, begins with a letter, dated 124 BCE, from the Jews in Jerusalem addressed to the Jews in Egypt, inviting them to a joint celebration of the Feast of Tabernacles. 2 Macc. 1.1 begins: 'From the Jews in Jerusalem and in the country of Judaea to their Jewish kinsmen in Egypt.' Then follows the greeting: 'Greeting and peace' (1.1b). Four prayers follow in the form of a wish (that is, prayer-wishes): 'May God prosper you and may he keep in mind the covenant he made'(1.2). In 2 Macc. 1.6 the letter affirms the senders' prayer: 'Here and now we are praying for you.' A narrative recalls a previous letter sent at a time of crisis; there

was a disaster, an answered prayer, and the preparations have been made for the new Feast of Tabernacles (1.9). There is no final greeting; just the date. When we come to the text of 1 Thessalonians we shall find several features similar to those in 2 Maccabees (but unfortunately no date!).

Two areas of research have thrown a great deal of light on the ancient letter. First, different kinds of letters have been identified and illustrated in epistolary study. A handbook on letter composition by Pseudo-Demetrius introduces examples of different styles. The Introduction runs:

> There are, then, twenty-one letter styles that we have come across. Perhaps time, since it is a highly gifted inventor of skills and theories, might produce more than these. But as far as we are concerned, there is no other type that properly pertains to the epistolary mode. Each of them is named after the form of style to which it belongs: friendly, commendatory, blaming, reproachful, consoling, censorious, admonishing, threatening, vituperative, praising, advisory, supplicatory, inquiring, responding, allegorical, accounting, accruing, apologetic, congratulatory, ironic, thankful. (Malherbe, 1986, No. 32)

What is interesting about this list and the illustrations which follow the list is their close relationship to oral communication. The letter is a means by which someone far distant becomes present as a living voice. Seneca makes this point in his extensive correspondence as mentor to the younger Lucilius. It is also obvious that more than one of these styles could be found in any one letter. 1 Thessalonians has been described as consolatory; and some of the phrases present in both Pseudo-Demetrius and Paul have that function. Some scholars use the term 'apologetic' of 1 Thessalonians (in the sense of answering charges made against him, as in a court of law); but we shall find less reason for that. The term 'friendly' certainly fits 1 Thessalonians, as does also the term 'commendatory'.

The reference to 'oral communication' and 'as in a court of law' leads into the second area of research on the ancient letter. The philosopher Aristotle distinguished between speaking in a court of law (proving a charge made in the past to be false), speaking in a political meeting (seeking a way forward for the future) and speaking in praise of a winner in the athletic games (congratulatory or commendatory); and he recognized and analysed the rhetorical techniques appropriate to these kinds of speech. In some way, such rhetorical techniques correspond with good common sense. The ordering of a speech will begin by building a relationship with the hearers, will then narrate the circumstances which have led to the speech, will point out the differences and agreements between various parties, and then present the key point which the speech is to make. Then the speaker will try to prove his or her case and finally round off with a summary of the key point. Rhetorical research gives technical names to each of these parts of the speech, as well as discussing the rules of logical progression and proof and the decoration of language to make it interesting and attractive.

A modern trend in the study of the Pauline letters is to ask how far this kind of common sense 'rhetoric' influenced Paul in the composition of his letters. So, modern commentaries often examine Pauline letters using terms such as Exordium (how the speaker builds a relationship with his hearers), Narratio (story-lines relevant to the main subject), Partitio (the main issue), Probatio (the proving of the case) and Peroratio (recapitulating the principal theme) – all terms which indicate the ordering of the material and inner relationship of the parts. Some of these terms carry a clear relevance to parts of 1 Thessalonians (Exordium, the fostering of relationship between writer and hearers, fits 1.2–10), Narratio follows with relevant narrative material (2.2 or 3.1–10). But the division of the text of 1 Thessalonians into the fully extended rhetorical ordering of the material has proved too difficult; and so far no division in either 1 or 2 Thessalonians has gained general agreement. For example, there are no less than three thanksgiving sections in the first part of 1 Thessalonians. So an obvious illustration of the problem in rhetorical ordering is the question. 'Where in 1 Thessalonians does the exordium end, and where does the narratio begin and end?'

But the question about rhetorical composition in the Pauline letters does not end there. Rhetorical techniques concern more than the ordering of material; they concern also the whole process of rhetorical persuasion: the appeal to reason (for example via syllogisms), to the character of the people involved, and to the use of the emotions; there is also the decoration of language with metaphors and similes and neat, memorable phrases. We shall comment on various examples of these arts of persuasion in the course of the commentary.

Before the research into epistolary and rhetorical considerations took a central place in Pauline studies, the structure of a letter was generally sought by finding the main themes of the letter (linguistic analysis), finding the main forms used (form-critical analysis) and seeing how the themes and the forms fitted together. Since in the case of 1 and 2 Thessalonians neither epistolary nor rhetorical studies have been able to reach entirely satisfactory conclusions (the question whether 1 Thessalonians is apologetic or advisory or complimentary is still not settled; nor is the relation between the exordium and the narratio; see Donfried, 2000, pp. 3–28); it seems best to employ also the older methods and to see what is still discovered through them. However, both epistolary and rhetorical studies will still be used to track the inner-relationships of the material within the two letters and the techniques of persuasion which emerge in the study of the text (Porter, pp. 533–85).

The key forms in 1 Thessalonians are the three thanksgivings (1.2–10, 2.13 and 3.9–10), the two sets of prayer-wishes (3.11–13; 5.23–24), each set serving as a conclusion to a main section of the letter (see the commentary on 4.1), and, as we have seen, the epistolary opening and conclusion (1.1; 5.25–28). As far as the letter's themes are concerned we shall be looking at the main terms – grace, peace, love, faith, hope, joy, holiness, brotherhood/sisterhood and many others, examining them in their epistolary and rhetorical roles, as well as in their theological and socio-historical functions.

The composition of 1 Thessalonians (and also of 2 Thessalonians) is best understood using all the new methods of research but with a close attention to the actual text. This reveals Paul creatively adapting epistolary forms in 1 Thessalonians, expanding the thanksgiving form, giving a friendly affirmation of mutual love and comfort, and, at the conclusion of each main section, offering prayers that summarise the concerns of each section and focus both sections on the purpose of holiness before God and at the parousia.

Finally, in this section on Pauline composition, 1 Thess. 5.27 ends that epistle by requiring of everyone in the Thessalonian Christian community a solemn oath to ensure the reading of the letter in public, without fear or favour (to 'all our fellow-Christians'). This is one of the few verses in 1 Thessalonians where Paul uses the singular 'I': 'I adjure you by the Lord.' In the rest of the letter Paul is associating himself with Silvanus and Timothy. It would seem that Paul occasionally wanted to isolate himself from his colleagues, where his personal feelings were deeply engaged (2.18; 3.5), and significantly where he personally required an oath from everyone

(5.27). Elsewhere, having included all three names as the senders of the letter, he uses the plural 'we', notably at the beginning in 1.2, and at 2.13 and 3.9 (the thanksgiving sections). Of course the use of the plural in ancient friendly correspondence did not necessarily mean a plurality of senders. A letter such as Seneca's fifth letter to Lucilius ('To his friend Lucilius, greeting'), commenting on the danger of causing ill-will by high standards, switches from singular to plural and back, especially marking the points where other people agree with him. However, the plural in 1 Thessalonians was probably also a way of avoiding an authoritarian impression, even perhaps a way of signalling the importance of mutuality. 1 Thess. 5.27 would then be, paradoxically, a requirement for inclusivity, even though made in the personal 'I' form.

'Without fear or favour' implies the inclusion of all, artisan or idle, sighted or blind, lame and handicapped, women or men, leaders or followers, literate or illiterate – especially the illiterate. The public reading of the letter would have given the high percentage of illiterates in Thessalonian society an opportunity to hear Paul's message. A very few slaves may well have been given the privilege of studying the art of reading and writing, perhaps in more than one language, but that would be the chosen few. The only way in which most of those present would have had access to Paul's words would have been via the public reading (Oestreich, pp. 225–45). That leads us on to the next introductory subject.

5. What does 'all our fellow-Christians' imply?

We said earlier that those who received 1 Thessalonians, whether Jew or Gentile, would have been wrestling with changes of commitment with incalculable consequences for their social and community lives. When Paul's letter was read to the whole Christian community, at least some of the hearers, perhaps even a majority of them, would formerly have been involved in traditional, pagan, Thessalonian or Roman, religious practices. That would not of course have been true of the Jews among them. They would have established their own way of living and surviving in a central Roman municipality without such an involvement in pagan religion; but, of course, having then associated themselves with the Christian community, they would have had their own problems with the family, local and institutional tensions which their conversion had caused.

That there were Jews in Thessalonica is certain, and that some were converted by Paul and Silvanus is also almost certain; there was probably, too, a synagogue in such a main provincial city. There is no archaeological evidence of a synagogue in Thessalonica in the time of Paul; but the problem involved in archaeological study of Thessalonica is that site work is limited by the presence of modern buildings on top of the ancient city. So it is difficult to be certain about Jewish life in Thessalonica in Paul's day. There would certainly have been Jews in Thessalonica; there would almost certainly have been converted Jews present to hear Paul's letter. Whether they continued to attend a synagogue or whether there was a synagogue in the city we do not know for sure.

Converted Jews apart, it would have been true of most of the others present at the reading of Paul's letter that they would have been, at some time or another, involved in the religious holidays and celebrations which a Graeco-Roman city provided. It would have been true of most if not all of the group of God-fearers (Blumenthal, pp. 96–105). God-fearers were not obliged to be believers in a single God; indeed the reason why they remained God-fearers and therefore on the fringe of Jewish society was in part beause they were not prepared to forgo all the options of religious ritual. Nevertheless, God-fearers, attracted to Judaism but unwilling to be circumcised or limit their religious options, were a fertile ground for missionary activities (Lieu, 1996, p. 129). As far as the latter was concerned conversion to Christianity did require of the God-fearers just that. What they may have been unwilling to forgo as God-fearers, they became obligated to forgo when converted to the God of Jesus Christ (1 Thess. 1.9–10). If it is difficult today to monitor in our own modern society the ripple effect of such conversions (see section 1 above), it is almost impossible to measure the consequences in an ancient society, especially one of which, despite all the research that has been carried out by classical and biblical scholars and archaeologists, only tiny fragments have proved recoverable.

A single example concerning a practical feature of ancient life relevant to 1 Thessalonians must suffice. Archaeological work in Pompeii, Herculaneum and Applontis (all of them in Italy), and in Corinth (in Greece, where Paul was when writing 1 Thessalonians) had led to the view that reasonably sized houses belonging to relatively affluent Christians provided the places for Christians to eat and worship together. As the archaeological studies have expanded, to this theory new studies have to be added from areas of ancient Corinth east of the Theatre. The options of work places and workshops and their second or third floors have begun to be considered as possibilities for such meeting places (Horrell, 2004, pp. 349–69).

Patterns of labour associations have been examined, both in relation to what constitutes poverty and in relation to issues of status, honour and worth (Meggitt, pp. 101–78). Details of ancient work associations have been gathered (Ascough, 2003, pp. 162–89; 2005, pp. 509–30), giving us an idea of their structure, membership, leadership, provisions for the death of members and discipline in the case of unruly behaviour. 1 Thessalonians pictures Paul and some of the converts involved at this level of artisan existence. Some of his comments could hardly have been made with any integrity or acceptance if he were not. Perhaps such artisan involvement did not extend to actually being a member of a leather-work association. (There is no evidence of Thessalonian associations contemporary with Paul, but that would not have prevented occasional working groups acting as joint survival strategies). So the work place may have been, to judge by the various references in 1 Thessalonians to hard work and labour, a common meeting ground at which Paul (and Silvanus) made contacts and converts. Whether their work place also offered a meeting place for a larger church community we can only guess.

Those comments on artisan involvement and life-style leave many important questions unanswered: were such association meetings a pattern followed by the church or did they actually become for some artisans 'church' meetings? Were converts individually made, or did they become Christ-followers as a group? Did the groups tend to be restricted to manual labourers and male workers? 1 Thessalonians poses many such questions, questions particularly concerning the 'ripple effect' of conversion: how acceptable locally was a work place with a religious ethos, and one which deliberately avoided the (frequent) holidays, festivals and feasts of local Roman religion – presumably affecting any (extended) family participation in them too? And were the workers committed to patronage? Were they slaves or freedmen, and how were these relationships affected by conversion? Was Paul's advice to 'aim at what is best for each other, and for all' a reasonable expectation (see also 1 Thess. 4.12)?

6. *Conversion and conflicts*

The conflicts caused by conversions in Thessalonica passed through several stages:

* stage 1 – the first arrival of the missionaries
* stage 2 – Paul's banishment
* stage 3 – Timothy's visit
* stage 4 – the writing of the letter.

A key Greek word in Thessalonians is *'thlipsis'* (which can mean pressure, affliction, oppression, distress, affliction, ills especially those besetting the people of God) and the word *'thlipsis'* in 1 Thessalonians relates to stage 1 at 1.6, to stage 3 at 3.3 and to stage 4 at 3.7 (accompanied by the word 'difficulties'). Stage 2 will be dealt with in the commentary on 2.14–16. *'Thlipsis'* is a general word, but there is no reason why it should always refer to the same experience, or be translated in exactly the same way in each temporal context. REB translates it 'grave suffering' in 1.6, in 3.3 'hardships'(of the Thessalonians) and in 3.7 'hardships' (of Paul and Barnabas). In 2 Thess. 1.4 it is translated 'troubles' and is accompanied by a word not found elsewhere in the Thessalonian correspondence, 'persecutions'. The related verb *'thlibomai'* is used in 3.4 of trouble which Paul had forecast, and is translated in the REB 'suffer hardship'. Paul also uses in 1 Thess. 2.2 the Greek word *'agon'* (context, struggle, strain, concern); it refers there to the missionaries' experience. REB translates this 'in the face of great opposition'. It would seem that both *'thlipsis'* and *'agon'* may refer to various stages: growing unease, conflict, and the ripple effect of conversion.

Conflict may also occur between groups; and group conflict can pass through various stages too (Still, pp. 268–85): a breach of etiquette or norm, mounting crisis between the various parties, attempts to resolve the crisis, then a resolution or more likely a lasting dispute, with for example, a minority closing its ranks and being given a tighter cohesion and exclusivity. In the case of a small group conscious of its breadline existence, it would need a great deal of mutual commitment to risk offending others groups who represented a potential market. Withdrawal from religious practices, especially state religion, would, as we have seen, involve family distress, social ostracism, or – at a political level – fear of superstition, mistrust of a foreign religion, misunderstandings (as in the confusion about God-fearers) or it could even lead to the charge of subversion. For God-fearers conflict might mean strained relationships with the synagogue and with those Jews who found Paul's teaching dangerous.

Is there any evidence that such conflicts led to oppression or persecution in Thessalonica? The clearest evidence in 1 Thessalonians of oppression (though not necessarily of any systematic attempt to root out the Church) is in 2.14–15. Thessalonian Christians have been ill-used by local townsfolk. They have shared the experience of the churches in Judaea; the Thessalonians had been treated by their local townsfolk as the Judaean churches were by theirs. Ill-treatment of the Judaean churches in the early period of the Christian Church is reasonably well documented (Bockmuehl, pp. 75–80). There was, according to Acts, an initial persecution by the Jews of early Christians in Judaea; and Paul provides personal testimony to this in the record of his pre-conversion zeal (Phil. 3.6). A second and later period included Herod Agrippa I's execution of James and arrest of Peter. What happened thereafter by way of persecution in the troubled times after Agrippa's death is hard to define, and the only evidence of persecution just prior to 1 Thessalonians is from a late, not always reliable, source. That leaves the expulsion of Paul and his colleagues from Philippi, then Thessalonica, and then Beroea – experiences which Paul took to be a thwarting of the divinely authorized Gentile mission. Besides those expulsions there is only the statement in 1 Thess. 2.14–15 that what the Thessalonian Christian had suffered stood comparison with the persecution of the churches in Judaea.

The Jewish, God-fearing and Gentile Christians were not alone in facing conflicts due to conversion. Paul's position was doubly problematic. As a converted Christian he was central to an outbreak of Christian fervour which he attributed to divine direction and which involved Gentile converts in hard decisions. He was also a Jew, given credence by some Jews but mistrusted by others. The latter saw his ideas and practices as deviant; for them his work could have been seen as an attack on ancestral customs, on family unity, as a questioning of their status as the people of God, and a challenge to the moral requirements of God. Such critics caused him intense pain. He had already experienced conflicts in Antioch and in Philippi. Now he had been separated from a young community and felt orphaned. To the hard work in which he was involved as a tent-maker was added mental torture and anguish of heart. What had been, in his view, a work of God (the success in Thessalonica) was, in the eyes of some, being emptied of its divine significance. No doubt there were Jews who suffered with him, for whom family pressures and leadership demands were inescapable.

There were other problems for Paul, his colleagues and his converts (1 Thess. 2.1–8). His sudden departure, his enforced silence and his extended absence must have allowed Jewish and Gentile criticisms and innuendos to mount, and possibly have given weight to slanderous accusations. Even the eventual letter might have encouraged his hearers to view Paul as holding too high a view of himself and his work. In holding himself up for imitation he might have been seen to be inviting admiration (Hooker-Stacey, 2003, p. 164).

The obverse of these factors would have been attempts in Thessalonica to discipline, restrain and discourage the converts. There would have been the distress and suffering caused by family, social and political disincentives. Paul attempted to diminish the effects of these on his new converts by advising them to 'live quietly', to keep a low profile, to attend to their own business, and thus to 'command the respect of those outside your number' (1 Thess. 4.11–12).

The conflicts for the converts as we have listed them are manifold. In the commentary we shall set these in their temporal, literary, sociological and theological contexts. But we cannot pretend to interpret in exact historical detail such a short letter, written against a background which exists for us only in fragmentary pieces of evidence. The main point is that there is already enough to warrant our initial suggestion in section 1: that we have a document here which opens up as a major human issue the personal and corporate cost of change.

7. *The nature of 2 Thessalonians*

We shall argue that 2 Thessalonians is an authentic Pauline letter and was written very shortly after 1 Thessalonians had been completed and dispatched. So 2 Thessalonians enables us to continue the discussion of the cost and danger of change, and other even more significant issues, into a further temporal stage.

Because the authenticity of 2 Thessalonians is a much-discussed subject we shall have to give space to some of the long-standing arguments. Some of the recent arguments against the authenticity of 2 Thessalonians can be dealt with immediately; the earlier and more substantial ones must be left until the theological and eschatological relationships of 1 and 2 Thessalonians have been considered. The most recent comparisons of the style of 2 Thessalonians with the style of generally recognized authentic Pauline letters have used GramCord (computer) studies. They claim that the style of 2 Thessalonians is un-Pauline. The analysis is unsatisfactory on two grounds. First, the analysis of the complexity of sentence structures is inaccurate: for example the thanksgiving section in 2 Thess. 1.3–13 is compared with the thanksgiving in 2 Cor. 1.3–7, whereas the actual thanksgiving motifs appear in 2 Corinthians as late in the text as 2 Cor. 1.11. If we compare 2 Thess. 1.3–13 with the whole thanksgiving in 2 Cor. 1.2–11, the statistical case for a difference in the complexity of sentence structures is too small for a decisive verdict. Second, the short length of 2 Thess. can only provide such small statistical figures that it would take only a single example (for example one due to the influence of the Septuagint in 2 Thessalonians) to alter the comparative results substantially. (By 'Septuagint' is meant a translation into Greek of major Jewish writings including Old Testament books.)

The other recent argument rests on rhetorical evidence: the rhetorical shape of 2 Thessalonians, which includes nine antitheses, suggests to some scholars a purpose for the letter incompatible with Pauline authorship. We shall argue that this is a misreading of the antitheses; as the commentary later will show, the stress of the antitheses is on the present attitude and future fate of the oppressors as contrasted with that of those who believe, an emphasis entirely compatible with Pauline argumentation elsewhere (see Phil. 1.28). It has also to be said that the text of 2 Thessalonians reflects the full rhetorical outline of materials even less well than 1 Thessalonians does.

So the recent stylistic and rhetorical arguments against the authenticity of 2 Thessalonians are not decisive. It is the older and longstanding ones which require the detailed attention. These are: the literary affinities between 1 and 2 Thessalonians, which include considerable agreements of order and content, together with major differences, raising questions concerning why Paul should have written both; the suspected tensions between the two letters with respect to eschatology and Christology; the reference to Paul's signature in 2 Thess. 3.17; and the possibility that 2 Thessalonians is pseudepigraphical (that is, ascribed to Paul although not written by him).

8. *The purpose of the Thessalonian letters*

So far we have given a general outline of 1 Thessalonians: there are the three thanksgivings, allowing the impression of a friendly affirmation of mutual love and comfort, of divine activity and of joyful, corporate persistence within difficult circumstances; and there are the two prayers (one at the conclusion of each of the letter's main sections), the first of which (3.11–13) prays for Paul's early return to Thessalonica, for the increase of mutual love there, and the affirming of their faith, so that the Lord may make them blameless and holy before God at the parousia (the main themes of the opening chapters); and the second prayer-wish (5.23) repeats the concern that the God of peace may make them holy and entire at the parousia (a focus for chs 4—5). So both of the prayer-wishes focus on the purpose of God and of the Lord that the Thessalonians should be holy at the parousia.

The friendly affirmation of mutual love and comfort, of divine activity and joyful corporate persistence in 1 Thess. 1.2–10 spells an important antidote to the disruption experienced by the converts, as do the constant references to the new kinships established there. It affirms also the conversion of the Thessalonians to the living God, to the expectation of the parousia, to the appearance of the Son raised by God from the dead, as the deliverer from the 'retribution to come' (1.10; later we shall question the translation and implications of the word 'retribution'). As Paul saw it, neither the resurrection of Christ, nor the significance of the resurrection for God's work of deliverance, nor the association of both with the parousia was in question among the Thessalonians. Nor was the relation of hope to the work of Christ, to his persistence, to his parousia and to the entrance before our God and Father a matter of doubt for the new converts (1.3; see the commentary). It is a community with those commitments which has become a celebrated, realized embodiment of the good news in Macedonia, Achaia and even further afield (1.6–8).

What of the second and the third thanksgivings? (Lambrecht, pp. 135–62) The second (2.13) links the acceptance by the Thessalonians of their divine vocation to God's kingdom (2.12) with the suffering they have endured (see section 6 above). This is an honoured parallel to that of the early Judaean Church, to the persecution of the prophets and to the death of Jesus, their Lord (see 5.10).The third thanksgiving (3.9) is a response to the good news brought to Paul by Timothy. There is no explicit suggestion that commitments described by Paul in 1.2–10 as features of their conversion state have in any way been lessened. There is an explicit plea that he might see them again and 'make good what is lacking in your faith' (3.10). Some have argued that there is an implicit note of concern as Paul rehearses their love and faith but makes no mention of their hope. Yet Paul has been advised that they stand firm (3.8; see also 5.8); and Paul, revivified by the news of their faith, makes the threefold prayer, ending with the prayer that their hearts may be firm so that they stand before God blameless at the parousia (see section 10 below) – if the REB translation is correct, 'with all those who are his own' (or, 'his holy ones'; 3.13).

There does not seem to have been a major failing or gap in their faith-commitments. Nevertheless, there was among the Thessalonians an element of insecurity, either because of the disruption of their lives through their conversion, or because of their new vocation to which they were not as yet wholly accustomed, or, it may be, because of both. Paul needs to address this anxiety (Marshall, 1990, p. 260). He recognizes it as quite a complex anxiety. It appears to be centred on their fate before the judgement of God at the parousia, an anxiety not altogether foreign to Paul's own consciousness (2.18–19; Rom. 9.3). That their fate might ultimately be outside God's work of salvation is signalled by the use of the word 'wrath', or 'retribution' (1.10; 5.9). Paul addresses this anxiety directly; he affirms that they are not designated for 'retribution, but for the full attainment of salvation' through Jesus Christ their Lord' (1 Thess. 5.9).

Various attempts have been made to define this anxiety more closely. Does 1 Thessalonians hint that among the Thessalonians there was a descent from hope towards despair, and if so what caused it? The constant barracking, ostracism and mockery of their neighbours? Or, was the unexpected death of some of their number (4.13) a shock which unnerved them, or which was turned by their neighours into a massive question mark against their faith, or seen as a sign or portent that God's day of judgement was upon them? (Nicholl, pp. 75–8) All those questions have been raised, and many more.

As we have seen, Paul's response (5.9) – and it is a response which emerges at various points in the letter – is that full salvation is attained 'through Jesus Christ our Lord', the deliverer, the strengthener both now and for the parousia, the one who shapes our lives toward the will and purpose of God, the one who died for us, so that we may all live together with him, whose grace is with us (see 1.10; 3.13; 4.2; 4.16–17; 5.23, 28). What the Thessalonians needed to add to their faith commitment was an awareness of the work of Jesus Christ, specifically in relation to divine judgement at the parousia. No doubt the death of their colleagues added to their anxiety, but it was an anxiety that went deep precisely because they took seriously the challenge to a holiness to which they were only lately becoming accustomed, in which the Holy Spirit engaged them (1.6; 3.13; 4.4–7). Would they be worthy of such a calling? And particularly would they be worthy at the parousia (2.12)? It was not that they doubted the resurrection, or the parousia, or the gift of the Spirit. Their calling involved a holiness which they could neither fully define, nor be certain they could embody, nor expect to match the moment of judgement. At least they had time to pursue the road to holiness. They were pursuing the way of Christ, and the way of the Spirit. At least they had time. Those who had died, had not. Their anxiety for them and for themselves was deep and unsettling. It was an anxiety that the deceased might be lost. Paul's response is a Christological one: at the parousia the one who is with them is God's deliverer, for God alone, the faithful God, can make those who belong to Christ holy (5.23), giving them, in their entire being, hope at the parousia of Jesus Christ. Christ has been their hope, throughout their entire Christian experience (5.23). As children of light, they live in and according to the light, so for them the day of the Lord does not overtake them as darkness (5.1–11). For those reasons they need not fear. They will not ultimately be outside the saving work of God at the time of judgement. God is trustworthy, and he has called them. 1 Thessalonians is not a lone witness to this Pauline response; Romans 4.23–25 and 10.8–13 deal with the same dilemma in a similar way. In both 1 Thessalonians and Romans the emphasis lies upon God as ultimately the faithful One, and in both the Resurrected One is with them at the last.

At that crucial point of Christology the patterns of past, present and future in 1 Thessalonians correspond with what we find in other expressions of Pauline theology. The visionary aspect of the descent of God's Son, the raising of the 'dead in Christ' and the rapture of 'those who are left' (1 Thess. 4.15–17) may be distinctive; but the conclusion to which the vision leads, that all will 'always be with him', is not (1 Thess. 4.11; see 2 Cor. 5.1–6). The same conclusion is reached in 1 Thess. 5.11, even if the 'day of the Lord' in 1 Thess. 5.1–11 is related to 'living in the light' in a way paralleled only in the post-Pauline tradition of the kingdom found in Ephesians (Eph. 5.1–18).

When we turn to 2 Thessalonians we find a very similar overall structure to that of 1 Thessalonians. We shall set out the details of this in the commentary. The comparative outline of the two letters shows that just as 1 Thessalonians is shaped by the thanksgiving and the prayer-wishes, the same is true of 2 Thesssalonians. There are similar opening verses in 2 Thessalonians to those in 1 Thessalonians. In both letters the REB reads: to those 'who belong to God our Father and the Lord Jesus Christ'. While that is part of what Paul intends, he and his colleagues are making in both letters the much richer claim: the letter is to those 'whose lives are defined by God our Father and the Lord Jesus Christ'. Everything that we have and are and can be has to be understood in that majestic and creative context, a context marked by 'grace and peace'. As in 1 Thessalonians, what follows the opening verses in 2 Thessalonians is a thanksgiving (see 1.3a) and an intercession, albeit an intercession more extended than in 1 Thessalonians (1.11a). The thanksgiving initially celebrates, as 1 Thessalonians does, the extraordinary features of the divinely formed community (2 Thess. 1.3–4), and then prays (1.11–12) that God may make them worthy of his call, fulfil their every good purpose and deed so the Lord Jesus may be glorified in them and they in him, by God's grace and the grace of the Lord Jesus. As in 1 Thessalonians there is also a second thanksgiving in 2 Thess. 2.13–16, immediately followed by a prayer to conclude the section. The content of the second thanksgiving is introduced by a kinship reference typical of the Thessalonian correspondence ('my friends, beloved by the Lord': 2 Thess. 2.13). The thanksgiving has strong similiarities with 1 Thess. 5.9, linking salvation with 'the Spirit who consecrates you' (or 'in the holiness of the spirit'); and adding a stress on the glory of the Lord typical of 2 Thessalonians (see 2 Thess. 1.10). The concluding prayer, introduced by a summary call to stand firm (2.15), invokes the Lord Jesus Christ himself and 'God our Father, who has shown us such love and in his grace has given us such unfailing encouragement and so sure a hope; may you be still encouraged and strengthened in every good deed and word' (2.16–17). The 'love' theme is strong in 2 Thessalonians (see 1.3; 2.10,13; 2.16–17).

So far, 2 Thessalonians and 1 Thessalonians match each other very closely in structure, style and content. In fact the similarities are so striking that it would be difficult, on the evidence so far, to see what need there could have been for 2 Thessalonians to be written at all. But within that similar structure there are three sections in 2 Thessalonians which are distinctive and explain why the letter is needed.

The first extends the thanksgiving to take in the experience of opposition ('under all the persecutions and troubles you endure'; 1.4c), adding two interpretations of that experience: first that God's righteous judgement is at work in it (1.5a), and second that God's intention is that the hearers should be deemed worthy of the kingdom. Those interpretations are explained (quite cautiously) in terms of God's righteousness: the respective fates of the persecuted and the persecutors are to be reversed; and the picture of the Lord's revelation is painted in the vivid colours and the deep perceptions of Isaiah 66. Against the background of disrupted lives and relationships God's work is seen in its manifold patterns of judgement and grace, in relation to Gentiles and God-fearers, and, in Paul's agonized awareness, Jews also. The persecutors in their present happy state are unwitting evidence and unwitting agents of the divine purpose, as the persecuted have been also in their obedience to Paul's witness. The extended thanksgiving is shaped in this way to bring out the contrast between those obedient to the good news and those who refuse to listen to God. Later on in 2 Thessalonians the alarm will be raised concerning the arrival of the day of the Lord. In this thanksgiving the question is: 'Who needs to fear the "day of the Lord"?' And the answer given is: the Thessalonian Christians can be confident of sharing in the glorification of their Lord. Despite all their anxieties and uncertainties about facing God at the parousia they will have by the grace of God and of Christ a share in that glory. It is those who persecute them, who refuse the good news, who should fear the day of the Lord. For them there will be a recompense for their disobedience. Throughout that opening thanksgiving, although Paul is handling issues concerning non-believers, we shall find that at no point does he commit himself to views about their fate that are incompatible with the teaching in Paul's other letters.

The second distinctive section takes for granted the pattern of

1 Thess. 4.11–16: the parousia of the Lord and the gathering to himself of all his people (2 Thess. 2.1). Paul is aware that from some source, probably from an external source and possibly connected with a supposed, forged letter, the Thessalonians have been told that the 'day of the Lord' has actually arrived (2.2). Here Paul clearly identifies the day of the Lord with the parousia of Christ, and recognizes that the news of its supposed arrival has caused terror and continued consternation. They had been disturbed earlier to think that their deceased colleagues might not be admitted to the final presence of Christ. Now the entire community faced that possibility, and confronted by the untimely arrival of the 'day of the Lord' feared for their own unreadiness and unworthiness. In 2 Thess. 1 Paul has pointed out that it is not the Thessalonian Christians who need fear the 'day of the Lord', but the disobedient; and in 2 Thess. 2 he takes up that theme again, distinguishing between the faithful and those who are deluded and 'doomed to destruction'. But Paul's task is also to show that the 'day of the Lord' cannot have come. As he had previously taught them, there will be clear, unmistakable and public events including ultimate blasphemy which must precede that day. They must precede that day because that is the testimony of Scripture, and because the personification of evil must rise first for Christ's final victory over the powers of the Satan to be achieved. Paul can also point to the Thessalonians' own experience of wickedness as even now at work (2.7a). They have been puzzled and worried by the signs of rebellion and 'wrath' around them. There is much worse to come. But the victory belongs to Christ, and the Thessalonian Christians are those chosen to find salvation and by the grace of God and of Christ they will attain it (2.13). This second distinctive section fits with the pattern of the parousia of the Lord and the gathering to himself of all his people in 1 Thess. 4.11–16 and a detailed study of 2 Thess. 2 confirms that there is no basic discrepancy between the two Thessalonian letters, and that 2 Thess. 2 faces a problem which arose after the receipt in Thessalonica of the first letter, requiring that a similar letter be sent to meet the new problem.

The third distinctive section in 2 Thessalonians opens the door much wider for a view of the Thessalonians' social situation. Paul sees the Thessalonians as a model form of successful witness, as against some of what he has found in Corinth. He prays that the Thessalonians will direct their hearts 'towards God's love and the steadfastness of Christ' (3.5). But a new situation has arisen, apparently quite distinct from what Paul had been dealing with in 2 Thess. 2. It concerns Paul's policy of artisan work and his own particular agenda for the life of the Christian community. Some have now deliberately chosen not to work, and Paul argues the case not only for rejecting such idleness but also for responsibility to rest on the shoulders of the Thessalonian community to find the appropriate form of discipline.

We have sufficient information now about the two letters to make some outline decisions about their purpose. Many other details remain to be covered, but they can be dealt with in the commentary. There have been five major difficulties in defining the relationship of 1 and 2 Thessalonians. First, they have so much material in common yet addressed different problems. Both factors have to be explained if Paul is to be regarded as author of both. A possible solution is that shortly after writing 1 Thessalonians Paul received oral information which caused him to write a further letter. The basis for his correspondence with the Thessalonians remained the same; hence the similarities of layout and content. But the false alarm regarding the day of the Lord required reminders of what Paul had originally taught them on that particular issue; and the problem of the wilful idlers needed immediate, corporate, pastoral attention. Second, it has been argued that their 'eschatologies' are incompatible. A response to that issue can point out that on the crucial matter addressed in both letters there is a major overlap of presentation between the two. Both deal with the question 'How could we possibly be worthy / holy at the parousia?'; both letters answer the question Christologically; and each approaches the issue at different historical moments. Neither the different approaches to the 'day of the Lord', nor the attitudes to non-Christians set up insurmountable obstacles to a common authorship. Third, Paul's signature at the end of 2 Thessalonians 'All genuine letters of mine bear the same signature' (3.17), is strange if it concludes a second letter to the Thessalonians. The verse was for a time a cornerstone of the hypothesis that 2 Thessalonians must have been written first. However, if in 2 Thess. 2.2 Paul was taking seriously the possibility of a hypothetical forged letter then the note about the signature would have been entirely appropriate. Fourth, it has been argued that the tone of 2 Thessalonians is so different from that of 1 Thessalonians that they could not both be from Paul's hand. Our comments on the thanksgiving, intercessions and prayer-wish sections of both letters show that the tone of the two letters is remarkably similar. Fifth, some scholars have made the relationship of 1 and 2 Thessalonians dependent on theories concerning the composite character of the letters as we have them, and on the possibility of post-Pauline additions. We shall argue that the case for 1 Thessalonians as a composite of two letters on the grounds that one part assumes a currrent persecution, the other does not, is undermined by our careful study of *'thlipsis'*; and 1 Thess. 2.14–17 is not a post-Pauline addition but integral to the presentation of the Thessalonians' suffering as an honourable parallel to that of the early Judaean Church.

All the five points require detailed work on the text of 1 and 2 Thessalonians; so the commentary must provide the supporting evidence for these answers to long-standing difficulties in assuming common authorship for both letters. Earlier, the more recent problems were answered. Now the remainder has reached an outline response. The greatest difficulty facing those who argue against the Pauline authorship of 2 Thessalonians is that of finding a context which would explain the need for the precise operation of copying an original document, a context which at the same time is sufficiently near to that of 1 Thessalonians to make the need to copy it a feasible response. The common authorship of 1 and 2 Thessalonians still probably remains the most satisfactory solution.

9. *The Thessalonian correspondence and social theory*

The provisional conclusion that 1 and 2 Thessalonians emerged within a relatively short period may not give us a long time frame in which to consider the developments in Thessalonica; it does however enable us to see a wider picture of the social order as Paul understood it in both 1 and 2 Thessalonians. There were apparently some richer members of the community, in addition to the artisan classes with which Paul identified himself. This gives particular significance to the extraordinary impression in 1 Thessalonians that the addressees include a labouring group with whom Paul closely identifies himself. Seen from the viewpoint of how the Pauline letters give shape to and reshape the relationships in Thessalonica, this voluntary identification of himself with manual labourers gives an interesting resonance to the theme of imitation in the letters. Writing from Corinth where the social relationships were more clearly marked, Paul ensures that, when 1 Thessalonians is read out publicly to everyone, those who live on the edge of poverty take central place in the Thessalonian community or communities. Some commentators on the Thessalonian letters employ the theory of love-patriarchalism to understand the charitable maintenance of the poor by their richer colleagues. By love-patriarchalism is meant: love-patriarchalism takes social differences for granted but ameliorates them through an obligation of respect and love, an obligation imposed upon those who are socially stronger. From the weaker are required subordination, fidelity and esteem (Theissen, p. 107). Paul, in 1 Thessalonians, makes that theory entirely inappropriate in that, when considering his own values, life-style and Christian commitment, he never identifies himself with the powerful but instead, emphatically and of his own free will, identifies himself with the labouring poor. In no Pauline letter does the authority of Paul become so subordinate to the imitation of Christ as is the case with 1 Thessalonians (Horrell, 1996, pp. 211–16).

The study of eschatology in the Thessalonian letters from the point of view of social theory has become in recent years of crucial importance. This is in part because eschatology as a study of Paul's world has been infected almost beyond recovery by the viruses of modernity. Our view of history and time has shaped the terms in which we understand the Pauline parousia and the 'day of the Lord'. From that standpoint alone, since the human relation to time varies from one culture to another, social theories and their relation to eschatology deserve particular attention. Social identity theory, a psychological theory of how social identity and belonging emerge, recognizes a distinctive orientation to the present and future as one feature of group awareness. For the Thessalonians that orientation becomes in 1 Thess. 4—5 a means of establishing and maintaining the identity of the Thessalonians as followers of Christ (Esler, pp. 1201–2). This social factor in the Thessalonian letters is one which has often in the past been submerged in individualistic interpretations of Paul. In view of the strained relationships caused by conversion, it is all the more important to be aware of the kind of belonging which social theory can reveal, its cognitive, emotional and relational factors. So, for example, faith can appear as a corporate reality in parts of the Thessalonian correspondence rather than only an individual commitment, or alternatively a community of trust may develop as well as personal trust in God. We shall explore these possibilities in the commentary. There are, however, three further considerations. First, the psychological basis of Social Identity Theory results in the treatment of the fundamental triad of faith, love and hope (1 Thess. 1.3; 2 Thess. 1.3) as identity descriptors, generating a favourable social identity for the group. Paul, as we shall see, does treat the triad as a means of identifying the character of the Thessalonian community, but establishes love not on the basis of the individual desire for fulfilment in a community, but as a fundamental reality, which for all the requirement of its actualization in practice, is rooted in the nature of God, and requires for embodiment, as in Paul's case the demeaning or even emptying of oneself. Second, the ongoing debate concerning Social Identity Theory (see Worchel, pp. 283–304 and Triandis, pp. 375–8) is increasingly interested not just in the in-group but in the extraordinary range of inter-group influences (see section 6 above) which need to be considered. In particular, this research by Worchel and Triandis, also Holmes and Elland (pp. 343–64) has explored the permeability of group boundaries, a permeability crucially important in Paul's letters. We shall note at least some examples of this in the commentary, especially in the area of the work place. Third, if it is true that the concerns of the in-group, as those destined for salvation and as against those heading for destruction, have constantly to be received in inter-group contexts, then the issues of what Paul understood God to be doing over and beyond the life of the local Christian community raises once more some of the central questions of eschatology (see Wainwright, pp. 274–82),

10. God and Christ in the Thessalonian letters

As we have seen, the opening of each of the letters defines the context of the letters as 'in our Father God' and 'in the Lord Jesus Christ'; and whereas the greeting in 1 Thessalonians is 'grace and peace', in 2 Thessalonians the source of that same greeting is described as 'from our Father God and the Lord Jesus Christ'. Grace is a fundamental aspect of the divine nature according to Paul. For Jew and Gentile grace makes salvation possible. Against the backdrop of a dishonouring of God, God extends his grace to the ungrateful, while still maintaining the holy and righteous demands of his honour. Such benificence contrasts with that of the tradition of the Emperor Augustus, both in Rome and across the Empire. God's grace expresses itself in the grace of Christ (1 Thess. 5.28; 2 Thess.

1.12; 3.18), whose gracious characteristic in the Thessalonian letters is endurance and perseverance. His apostle, reflecting this grace, imitates that perseverance and reflects that grace in his addresses to the Christian community (1 Thess. 2.11).

Much has been made of the occasions in 2 Thessalonians where the order of God and Christ is reversed. 2 Thess. 2.16 begins the prayer-wish with the reversed order: 'May our Lord Jesus Christ himself and God our Father . . .' The reasons for this order are not far to seek. The prayer-wish concludes the detailed discussion of the 'day of the Lord' and the stress on the glory to be shared with the Lord Jesus Christ (2.14). The prayer-wish also continues with participles (or in the REB with clauses) illustrating God's love and grace. As in every case there are balancing factors, so that in both epistles the balance of the work of God and of Christ is maintained.

A study of the phrase 'the living and true God' (1 Thess. 1.9) enables us to explore that balance. The Gentiles and God-fearers are involved in commitment both to God and in awaiting his Son from heaven. That commitment to Christ makes it impossible for the God-fearers to continue with any understanding of God which is not monotheistic. With that commitment a new people of God emerges who acknowledge Christ as Lord. God is also seen active in the creating of a new people marked by the Holy Spirit's work (1 Thess. 1.6), inclusive of Gentiles (1.4,9; see Gal. 3.1–6) and there-fore threatening any Jewish claim to racial exclusivity. He is the One who raised his Son from among the dead (1.10), to be the deliverer of his people, so they may live always together with him (1 Thess. 5.11). The Lord's deliverance of his people from evil also embodies the same trustworthiness as does God's bringing of his people to salvation (1 Thess. 5.24; 2 Thess. 3.3). There is an unusual use of the definite article 'the' before God in 2 Thess. 1.12, whereas in the same verse there is no definite article before 'Lord Jesus Christ'. Some have suggested that this makes 'Lord Jesus Christ' an aspect of 'Our God'. The phrase is in all respects parallel to 2 Thess 1.2, except that in 1.12 the pronoun 'of us' is added to God but not to 'Lord Jesus Christ'. The addition of the definite article was prob-ably caused by the personal pronoun used with God and the omis-sion of the pronoun with 'Lord' (contrast 2 Thess. 2.1, 14, 16; 3.6). There is therefore no case to be made for regarding 'Lord' in 1.12 as an aspect of God. The intertwining of the influences of God and the Lord are multiple and illuminating.

The means of salvation involves imitation and participation. The community imitates Paul as they also imitate the Lord (1 Thess. 1.8); the result is a vibrant community as it receives the word. Participation involves a larger context than imitation. The context takes us back to the creation of humanity in the image of God, and loss of the divine glory there. Through the death of Jesus Christ who shares in that death, God opens the possibility of new life and a share in the divine glory (see 2 Thess. 2.14; see 2 Cor. 3.18; 4.4). Sharing in that death requires a persistent dying. Christ's persistence (2 Thess. 3.4) becomes therefore a further aspect of that same interchange, as also does Christ's trustworthiness (see 'the faith of Christ' in Gal. 2.20). These considerations shed some light on the observation that terms used of God are used of Christ in 2 Thessalonians. The interchange of terms is inevitable since their work is so interrelated.

The use of the word 'wrath' in 1 Thessalonians contrasts with the election of God's people to salvation (1 Thess. 5.9), and rather than suggesting a feature of the divine work, it seems in 1 Thessalonians to demarcate that area which is outside God's saving work: the chaotic patterns of life, organization and relationship which humanity knows in its isolation from the life-giving God. In 2 Thessalonians this is developed to include the eventual outcome of that isolation in various aspects of death.

Fundamental to the nature of God and his creation is love (2 Thess. 3.5). Integral with Paul's treatment of the parousia is that to be loved by Christ is to be loved by God also (1 Thess. 1.4; 2 Thess. 2.13). Love is the common activity of God and the Lord Jesus by which salvation becomes possible. In practical terms also love may open the way for Paul to visit the Thessalonians again; it may increase the mutual love of the Thessalonians (1 Thess. 2.11–13). Strengthening may come from both the Lord Jesus and the Father 'who has shown us such love' (2 Thess. 2.16). Other aspects of the divine love will become apparent in the next section on the Thessalonian triad.

The shared glory of God in his majesty (1 Thess. 2.12) and of Christ in his transcendence is particularly evident in 2 Thessalonians (see 1.10, 12; 3.1). This marks the victory of Christ over evil, and the assured goal for those who are called through Paul's gospel (2 Thess. 2.14).

11. *The function of the recurring triad*

The triad 'faith', 'love', 'hope' (in that order), appears in 1 Thess. 1.3; 5.8. In the better-known order it is found in 1 Cor. 13: 'faith','hope', 'love'. The origin and significance of this Triad has been the subject of many monographs and studies. Did Paul originate the triad, and if so, when and why? In 1 Thessalonians the three words, each with a qualifying word, designate the divinely inaugurated, vibrant community which Paul celebrates. It could well be that this marks the inauguration and the purpose of the triad. Other Thessalonian passages may point in that direction. In 1 Thess. 5.8, Paul picks up the tradition of Isa. 59.9 and Wisd. 5.18 and links faith and love together, as he does also in 1 Thess. 3.6 and in 2 Thess. 1.3. It has been suggested that the omission of 'hope' in the two latter passages betrays a sense that the Thessalonians have lost the hope which characterized their early conversion experience. More likely in the light of the history of the three words is that 'love' and 'faith' were the earlier association, and 'hope' was an addition for the purpose of formulating the Thessalonian Christian community's character (Söding, pp. 67–220). In 1 Cor. 13 it is 'love' which is the central quality; in Gal. 5.6 'faith' and 'love' become a crucial for-mula; in 2 Cor. 13. 11, 13 'peace' and 'grace' are the companions of 'love'; and in Eph. 6.13–18 the Isaianic tradition was provided with several other key Pauline terms. 'Remembrance' too provides in 1 Thess. 3 a third element of a triad.

'Love' is a central Pauline term in the Thessalonian correspon-dence in relation to God and Christ, to Paul as a model for imitation and to the Thessalonians with respect to their relationships inside and outside the Christian community. Many dangers are inherent in the word, where 'love' becomes in practice enforcing a private ideology, enslaving and monopolizing the other person using various forms of manipulation and torture. They are dangers which contribute to the complexity of relationships which we noted in section 1. These are confronted by Paul in the Thessalonian letters, through his insistence on mutuality and on the many forms of 'death' which are the divine means of recovering true life (Wischmeyer, pp. 116–30).

So far we have described the triad in terms of words and terms. In the commentary we shall be looking at the many ways in which the three Greek terms are used by Paul. So for example '*pistis*' the greek word for 'faith' will be seen sometimes as carrying a stress on 'faithfulness', sometimes on 'loyalty', sometimes on 'commitment', sometimes on 'belief', sometimes on 'trust'. This will have the benefit of identifying the many practical features of Christian living which contribute together to make a community vibrant and the many ways in which God's work in Jesus Christ can be seen as effective in the community's life in worship, mutual care and service, offering an alternative to the maelstrom of misunderstanding that threatens to engulf ourselves and our communities when change threatens.

COMMENTARIES

1 Thessalonians
PART ONE

The address and greeting
1.1

V. 1 *From Paul, Silvanus, and Timothy* introduces no ordinary greeting. It carries its own history. For Paul will shortly indicate that he has considerable information about what has been happening among churches in Macedonia and Achaia, while having himself (according to Acts) contact only with Beroea and Athens (which he reached by sea from Pydna) and Corinth. Concerning Silvanus' movements, on the other hand, Acts is less clear. The congregation in Beroea made sure that Silvanus and Timothy remained behind in Beroea, and the instructions that they were to follow Paul to Athens were only received when those who accompanied Paul to Athens returned. How quickly Timothy followed we can only judge from 1 Thess. 3.1–2, where we understand that he was despatched (back?) to Thessalonica. Then, according to Acts, Silvanus and Timothy came down from Macedonia together and joined Paul in Corinth (Introduction, section 2). That leaves probably several months, if Acts is to be believed, when Silvanus was still in Macedonia and presumably not just kicking his heels, although probably keeping clear of Thessalonica. So he had ample opportunity to judge the impact which events in Thessalonica had had on the surrounding areas, and no doubt would have shared that with Paul when the two of them, Timothy and himself, rejoined Paul there (Barrett, p. 865). Almost certainly the Thessalonians knew what Silvanus had suffered, along with Paul, in Philippi (see 1 Thess. 2.2), since the Philippians had sent financial support to the missioners in Thessalonica in view of those events (see Phil. 1.19–20; 4.16).

Meanwhile Timothy, as a junior colleague, not so publicly involved in the initial work in Thessalonica, could act on

3

Paul's behalf to make contact with the Christian community in Thessalonica without attracting the kind of trouble which Paul and Silvanus aroused. Timothy, according to Acts, was from Lystra, son of a Jewish Christian mother and a Gentile father, and circumcised on Paul's authority so that he could accompany him on his missionary work (Acts 16.1–3). That Timothy's work as a go-between did not always bring him approval from his hosts, nor necessarily unquestioning confidence from Paul, is a feature of the Corinthian correspondence (see 1 Cor. 4.17–21). That the news he brought back to Paul from Thessalonica (1 Thess. 3.6–10) may not have been entirely up-to-date when he delivered it (see 2 Thess. 2.2) was probably in no way Timothy's fault.

Then there is Paul himself, the main author of the letter, but choosing to write it in the name of all three of them. That he should have done so (see Introduction section 4) may have had much to do both with his state of mind and his purpose in sending the letter. He had felt bereft, and admits that in the most personal forms of address (1 Thess. 3.5). The arrival of Silvanus and Timothy in Corinth had given him encouragement both because of the news that Timothy brought and because the three of them were together again – and Paul's immediate circumstances in Corinth may not have been altogether happy (2 Thess. 3.2). The purpose of 1 Thessalonians also applauds mutuality, especially mutuality of concern, comfort and love; and the inclusion of all three of them – himself, Silvanus and Timothy – at the beginning of the letter may well be an indication of what is to come in the rest of the letter; the work of mission is a corporate enterprise and involves all committed to it.

So we picture Paul, along with Silvanus and Timothy, as he dictates the letter. While he sat or paced around, who took notes of what he said, and who wrote up the final draft? Both of these techniques were specialized and required training. The notes would be made on a wax tablet and would need to have been virtually complete, perhaps even in a stenographic form. (And was the wax tablet kept, or smoothed off for re-use?) The copying out of a finished text on papyrus would be time-consuming and require a thorough knowledge of the subject. Who in Corinth could provide that? The name of Silvanus appears in 1 Pet. 5.12 with a broad hint in the text that Silvanus had been the amanuensis, and oddities in both 1 Thessalonians and 1 Peter have been thought to confirm that. If Silvanus provided that service for Paul, and presumably completed the task, interesting questions arise. Was Paul aware of Silvanus' skill when he chose him as a travelling companion to enter Syria and Cilicia, and parted company with Barnabas and Mark. If he was, surely Paul would have made use of that facility at an earlier stage of their travels, although perhaps to try out his skills in personal letters, and not necessarily to produce a letter to a church.

Paul must have given this major letter a great deal of thought. He had thought through the pastoral issues involved: should he name names, or because the letter was specifically for all to hear (see Introduction section 5) ensure that everyone felt addressed? He was an orator, but knew that to transfer his words to papyrus was a different task. The basic techniques involved in transferring the oral to the written had been worked at from the time of Homer onwards: you set down important phrases, words that might escape you or be difficult to spell, on scraps of dispensable material. What was written must also be clear when it was read aloud, and the association of words on the page would need to be the useful associations for hearing the message (that becomes an important principle in interpreting 1 Thess. 1). And of course the outline must be clear, and clearly marked, and the direction of the material recognizable (see Introduction, section 4 on the relation of Paul's letter to epistolary and rhetorical studies). Perhaps a basic outline was available to Silvanus. And did Timothy have any opportunity to comment? We can only surmise the answers here. What is clear is that the letter was thoroughly thought through, and committed to papyrus with an accuracy that satisfied Paul. Such a result, in an original enterprise, required many different skills. Some of the most creative moments in early Church history were the result of careful planning; not all were 'off the cuff'.

The letter was *to the church of the Thessalonians*, not 'in Thessalonica' as in other letters, where Paul usually specifies the place name. Why the people of the locality should qualify the word 'church' here, as they do also in 2 Thess. 1.1, is a matter for conjecture. The phrase certainly is consonant with the way in which the early verses of both letters make the people's experience and response the focus of events. 'Church' as used here lacks many of its modern associations. Just how many of those associations were missing, the shortness of the letters does not permit us to know; there is no specific mention in these letters of Baptism or Lord's Supper, but it is hard to imagine Paul giving no instruction regarding these, however brief a time he was with them. One of the other associations missing in the Thessalonian epistles is the Church as a unity of geographically separate congregations. That Paul uses the plural 'churches of God' in 2.14 is probably significant; the churches in Judaea (for the plural see also 2 Thess. 1.4; Gal. 1.1, 22; 1 Cor. 7.17; 11.16, 22; 14.33, 34; 16.1, 19; Rom. 16.4, 16) were designated specially as 'churches of God which are in Judaea in Christ Jesus' (see Introduction, section 10). The plural in 2.14 is particularly interesting because they could quite naturally have been spoken of as united in their persecution, as Paul implies in 1 Cor. 15.9: 'I persecuted the church of God'. Gatherings of early Christians could be thought of in the early stages as groups, as communities or assemblies or associations deriving their unity from Christ (see the questions posed at the end of Introduction section 5). So the use of 'church' of the Thessalonian Christians is important, even if it lacks the place name. Alternative plural phrases were available for designating such groups or associations. Where Paul wishes in 1 Thessalonians to refer to Christians in different parts of the Roman Empire he has the option of referring to them as 'those who are believers' (1.7). Whatever picture Paul has of the Thessalonian Christians in 1.1 he gives them the name of 'church' and sees them potentially as those who could gather together in a single place of assembly to listen together to the reading of his letter (5.27). The addition at 1.1 of 'in *God the Father and the Lord Jesus Christ*' establishes the Thessalonians' place within the total pattern of divine creation and redemption, along with all those who believe, as it also provides a foundation for the election and call of the vibrant young community Paul is about to describe (on the significance of their election to salvation as the firstfruits in Macedonia pointing to the great final ingathering see 1 Thess. 1.7 and the commentary on 2 Thess. 2.13). The REB translation uses the phrase 'belong to God the Father' which expresses a part of the verse's meaning but not its totality.

Grace to you and peace. This distinctively Christian greeting (see also the farewell in 5.28 with the addition 'of our Lord Jesus Christ') involves in human relationships the central term used regarding the nature of God and the Lord Jesus Christ (see Introduction section 10). The impact of that greeting is not immediately obvious to us. We are used to 'grace' as a general term related to 'graciousness'. But the Greek word *'charis'* had a different background, especially when it was used of human relationships. It belonged to the framework of ancient culture where generosity laid on the receiver the responsibility of a response (Harrison, pp. 345–52). There are hints of this background in the New Testament. In a classic passage on *'charis'* and the 'Collection for the Saints' Paul comments: 'At the moment your surplus meets their need, but one day your need may be met from their surplus. The aim is equality' (2 Cor. 8.14). The passage is about 'generosity' (or as the REB translates *'charis'* in 8.4, 6, 7 'generous service'), but not quite in the way we normally use the word. It is actually about the generosity of our Lord Jesus Christ (8.9), that 'through his poverty you might become rich', a pattern in which we may participate, and discover there not only the potential for sharing resources, but an increasing thanksgiving to God (another way Paul uses *'charis'*: 'Thanks be to God for his gift beyond praise'; 2 Cor. 9.15). So the initial greeting in 1 Thess. 1.1 and the final farewell are not only much more than a replacement for a traditional letter opening *'chairein'* ('Hail'); it has a surprising depth: 'Grace to you' wishes you the abundant riches and open responsiveness of life in Christ – a warm and welcoming greeting, whose determinative and unlimited character has yet to be fully understood by its recipients (ancient or modern).

To this Paul adds 'and peace'. We are familiar with the background to 'peace' in the Hebrew word *'shalom'*: wholeness, health, prosperity, personal and corporate. 1 Thess. 5.23 extends that meaning beyond its normal limits in the letter's concluding prayer. As we shall see later in the commentary, 5.23 is a prayer that the God of peace will endow us with the wholeness of life in Christ, that holiness which fulfils every part of being, in all the ways the letter will try to explore. And that includes the mutual recognition of each other identified in 5.26 as 'the kiss of peace'. That simple act of mutuality requires no particular formality or, for that matter, informality. What it says is said in its simplicity.

The first thanksgiving
1.2–10

V. 2 *We always thank God for you all* is the central pillar of the structure Paul now builds. One of the curious differences between the original Greek text and the modern English translation is that the original Greek text was intended to be heard but flows along unimpeded, whereas the modern English translation, when it, too, is intended to be read aloud and heard in public, has to be broken up into small segments. That is the case with the REB translation of 1 Thess. 1.2–10. That means that one of our tasks in commenting on this passage is to show where the links are, links which the segmented nature of a modern translation leaves to the hearer to provide. In the Greek the links are, on the whole, evident as the text flows along. There is one important exception, and to that we shall come in due course.

The simplest way to see the section as a whole is to set out the REB translation, but highlighting in bold words and phrases which indicate links, and underlining examples where attention to the whole edifice is easier with a more literal translation, or where an alternative Greek text is to be preferred.

We always thank God **whenever** we pray for you all   v. 2
recollecting how your faith has shown itself in action,   v. 3
     your love in labour,
     and your hope of our Lord Jesus Christ in perseverance
          <u>at the presence of our God and Father;</u>
knowing my dear friends, beloved of God,   v. 4
     that God has chosen you,
       how our good news <u>occurred with respect to you</u>   v. 5
       <u>not in word alone, but also</u> with power
       namely with the Holy Spirit <u>and full</u> conviction,
as you know <u>what kind of people we turned out</u>
  <u>to be among you</u> for your sake
      and indeed <u>you became our imitators and</u>
       <u>imitators of the Lord,</u>   v. 6
        having welcomed the message
        in grave suffering with the Holy Spirit's joy
and so you became a model for all believers in
  Macedonia and Achaia   v. 7
     for from you the word of the Lord had rung out   v. 8
      and not in Macedonia and Achaia alone,
      rather, everywhere your faith in respect of
       God <u>had gone out</u>
     so <u>we need not speak of anything about you,</u>   v. 9
for they tell our reception with you:
     how you turned <u>to God</u> from idols <u>to serve</u> the
      true and living God
     and to wait expectantly for his Son from heaven   v. 10
      whom he raised from dead
     Jesus, the one delivering us from the coming <u>wrath</u>.

This outline reveals six features of the opening chapter: first, the whole chapter appears to be one of thankful recollection of the early days of the visit of Paul and Silvanus to Thessalonica; second, Paul's knowledge is of how the good news became effective in Thessalonica (v. 4), and that is balanced by the hearers' knowledge of the kind of people the missionaries turned out to be (v. 5d); third, this balance is then restated in terms of an imitation (v. 6) – the Thessalonians imitate what they saw in Paul, and what both they and Paul see in their Lord, imitating and participating in his joy in suffering; fourth, this vibrant experience constituted a powerful testimony (v. 8); fifth, it was a testimony which confirmed what both Paul and the Thessalonians knew, concerning the Thessalonians' conversion to and serving of the living God, as Gentiles and God-fearers leaving their former idols (v. 9); and sixth, they await the redemptive work of God in his risen Son who is bringing deliverance at the last.

The centre of the chapter is therefore what happened in Thessalonica. Among the sections underlined in the outline above are the words 'occurred' v. 5a, 'turned out to be' v. 5d, 'became' v. 6, 'became' v. 7 (Heidegger). These all come from the same Greek word; they mark the event which is celebrated. The features of that event are multiple: the triad and its practical results, God's election, the Holy Spirit's work, the model of the missionaries derived from their Lord, their gospel, its effectiveness, the testimony to Macedonia and Achaia, the testimony to the threefold change in the Gentiles and God-fearers, and the content of that change. A living event has taken place with those dynamic, interrelated factors. A vibrant community has come into being. No wonder Paul looks back with thankful recollection.

There is, however, more to the chapter than an event. The event was a conversion that meant for the converts the beginning of a story which, through imitation of and participation in Christ, promised hope in the presence of God the Father. Against that background Paul's task in the letter was to convince the converts that the promised hope could become at the parousia of the Lord a realized reality for them all, despite all their anxieties, fears and uncertainties about themselves and their colleagues.

1 Thess. 1.1–10 awakens thoughts of Rudolf Otto's seminal work on *The Idea of the Holy*. It is about real experiences, occasioned by that which is Other; it is about the experience of the Holy. It is a powerful, clear context; and we can now look at the detail of the

chapter without losing sight of Paul's strategy (Crowder, pp. 22–47).

V. 3 This contains the triad, faith, love, hope (see Introduction, section 11): . . . *your faith has shown itself in action, your love in labour, and your hope of our Lord Jesus Christ in perseverance.* The REB translation 'faith has shown itself in action' is interesting in that it answers the question, 'What has faith to do with works?'; but it answers the question before it is asked. And here that particular question is not asked. It is asked in later Pauline correspondence, and answered in the phrase: 'faith expressing itself through love' (Gal. 5.6). In 1 Thessalonians the word translated faith, *'pistis'*, has some unexpected settings, as we have already seen in 1.8. In 1.8 the total event which Paul celebrates becomes a powerful testimony; the testimony is not 'faith contrasted with works'; it is the amazing, corporate experience in which the gospel, its effectiveness, the Spirit, the faith-commitment, the missionaries, joyful in their tribulation, and their imitators come together. *'Pistis'* in 1.8 is a corporate faith-event. The word translated 'action' is in the Greek *'ergon'*. In 5.12 it belongs in the context of hard work by the leadership to be valued in the common search for peace. In 4.12 it is the manual labour which belongs with the model Paul so strongly commends. We cannot be sure if Paul envisaged the relationship of those verses. A conclusion might be: 1.3 is recollecting the 'practical outworking of common faith-commitment'. It is an event with an extended character.

The second of the triad, 'your love in labour', picks up accurately the link in the Thessalonian letters between 'love' that is the foundation of all life (see Introduction, section 11) and its painful working out in daily life. 2 Thess. 3.4–8 illuminates that relationship. There is an immediacy and a contemporary quality to love. It belongs to the present, and is what we are doing in the present. There is a relational aspect, a bonding and commonality. It is, above all, that which enables the stranger to find a home, the uprooted to dare to put down roots again and the lonely to feel that they belong and can become a part of the 'beloved of God' (1 Thess. 1.4). There is a universal aspect that can be recognized, and valued wherever and whenever it is found (see 1 Thess. 4.12). It can be worked at and improved (1 Thess. 4.9–12). Its costliness is part of the model which Paul discovered in God's Son and became a part of the model which the Thessalonians followed. The relationship between that Pauline model in 1 Thess. 2 and 1 Cor. 13.4–7 is not difficult to find. Paul is speaking of 'love in painful service'. What is not clear is whether in the phrase in 1.3 love is motivation, inspiration, enablement or intention, or, as the above examples suggest, all four.

The final part of the triad, 'your hope of our Lord Jesus Christ in perseverance' is noteworthy for its additional features. In 5.8 hope is 'hope for salvation'; in 2.19, hope, along with joy and a triumphal crown, is Paul's way of valuing the Thessalonian converts when 'we stand before our Lord Jesus at his coming'. The prayer in 2 Thess. 2.16 puts a 'sure hope' alongside Jesus Christ and the God who has shown us such love; the prayer is that the Thessalonians will find the encouragement there to every good deed and word. There is a great deal in classical literature concerning hope; most famously it appears in Pindar's poetry written for declamation after outstanding performances at the Games. But it is a different hope from Paul's. The Pauline hope faces the terrifying possibilities that lie outside the redemptive activity of God, what Paul calls 'wrath', what the REB calls 'retribution' in 1 Thess. 1.10, and facing that terror affirms Jesus Christ as the redemptive power of God to shield and save from such a fate.

It is at this point that 1 Thess. 1 presents us with a difficult problem of interpretation. The REB takes the phrase 'before our God and Father' in 1.3 from its position in the Greek text and places it next to 'we continually call to mind'. Before God is where we raise our prayers and recollection. The Greek text places the phrase after 'the hope of our Lord Jesus Christ in perseverance'. Our hope in Christ is as we share his perseverance (see 2 Thess. 3.5) before the judgement seat of God. The two arguments which make the second alternative preferable are: that is how the text would probably have been heard (as distinct from it being studied as a written text); and the second alternative fits most closely with the argument of 1 Thess. 1 as we have outlined it.

What Paul recollects, under the heading of the triad, is therefore: a powerful range of effects from a corporate faith-commitment in Thessalonica, the costly daily life of love there to which testimony has been given, and their hope in Christ, as they share his perseverance, when it comes to the judgement seat of God.

V. 4 Knowing, *my dear friends, beloved by God* gives us two keys to this and the following chapter. The first is that Paul is building up a mutually attested fund of knowledge regarding what happened when the missionaries began their work in Thessalonica, of their 'reception' there. He begins with what he knows of those events himself; he then turns to what the Thessalonians know of them (v. 5d 'as you know what kind of people we were among you'). In the following chapter, 1 Thess. 2.1–11, a similar pattern continues: the Greek word *'oidate'* ('you know') appears four times (2.1, 2, 5, 11), each time in relation to the missionaries' 'reception', behaviour, actions and the associated events. The events associated with the missionaries' 'reception' become the main reference point; and the events are marked by one particular Greek verb 'to happen' (see above: v. 5a 'occurred', v. 5d 'were'; v. 6 and v. 7 'became'; and see 2.1, 7, 10). These were recalled as actual events and were events of great significance.

The second key to v. 4 and the subsequent chapters is Paul's use of 'dear friends' (literally 'brothers'). This reappears at 2.1, 9, 14; 3.7; 4.1, 10, 13; 5.1, 4, 12, 14, 25, 26, 27 – remarkably frequent for such a short letter. There is a process here taking place of rebuilding kinship ties. The kinship is powerfully expressed: *beloved by God* (1.4); it is given deep roots (2.3–7); couched in emotionally powerful language (2.8); strengthened by self-offering, concern and love (2.9); it is expressed in metaphor (2.7, 11), established further by a new shared vision (2.19); taking those who share in sympathy, tragedy and understanding beyond what human limits prescribe (4.18; 5.11); it reaches new levels of mutuality (3.12; 4.9) and common trust (3.7), of general responsibility and shared labour (4.1–11). For those whose lives had been turned upside down by the events at the missionaries' reception, whose relationships in the households, at work and in the neighbourhood had been dislocated, here was an actuality to which Paul could refer: unbearable tensions were being transformed in a new kind of community – the people of God, reshaped with relationships that established deeper foundations than are usual in common life.

Paul ascribed that new development and their place as 'my dear friends, beloved of God' to divine choice: *he has chosen you* (v. 4b). What is implied in this divine 'choice'? Certainly a gracious and loving act of God, such as brought Israel into being and now brings into being a reshaped people of God; probably to the divine choice of non-Jews. The word Paul uses in 1 Thess. 1.4 relates specifically to the history of the Jewish people. In that respect the emphasis is different from parallels in Romans. There God's work of salvation is designated by the choice of Isaac's line (Rom. 9.11), of a remnant

(11.5), of a chosen few (11.7), a choice with mercy as its ultimate aim (11.28). Now Gentiles have been chosen; they are the means by which God's work of salvation may be more widely effective. 2 Thess. 2.14 makes precisely that point in a similar context (if we take the most likely text – 'firstfruits', and not as in the REB 'from the beginning of time' (see the commentary on that passage): 'my friends beloved by the Lord, God chose you as firstfruits for salvation in holiness of spirit and trust in truth'. Parallel to, and overlapping with, the divine choice is the divine call, not a so-called 'effectual call' (a call in which God ensures a positive response), but one aided by the Spirit, carrying with it the responsibility to be worthy of the kingdom through trust in the trustworthy God (1 Thess. 2.12; 4.7; 5.24), a call associated with the gospel (2 Thess. 2.14).

According to the REB, 1 Thess. 1.5 gives a reason for God's election and call: *because when we brought you the gospel we did not bring it in mere words.* That is a possible translation. But, more likely, as in the outline given earlier, 1.5 expounds the actual circumstances of the divine choice: 'how our good news occurred with respect to you, not in word alone . . .'. Paul is concerned to expound the actual cirumstances of the divine choice; and he continues to do that in 1.5cd: 'As you know what kind of people we were among you for your sake' and 'indeed you became our imitators and imitators of the Lord'. The circumstances are important as facts, not as causes. The cause is divine; the cause of everything that happened is the divine activity present within the events.

That is evident in v. 5bc: 'how our good news occurred with respect to you, not in word alone but with power, namely with the Holy Spirit and full conviction'. This differs from the REB in several respects, but fundamentally because almost certainly the original text has no preposition before the words 'full conviction', whereas the REB translation assumes such a preposition. The effect of this absence of a preposition before 'full conviction' is that 'Holy Spirit' and 'full conviction' belong together, thus providing an important definition of 'power'. Translated in that way v. 5 refers not just to those who preached the gospel, but to the remarkable circumstances in which that proclamation of the word occurred. It was a 'power-filled' situation in which the Holy Spirit was evident, giving full conviction (presumably both to speakers and to listeners), or to speakers with evident response from the listeners (see v. 6) and requiring a continuing response (see 4.7–8).

13

The mutuality experienced in those extraordinary circumstances is then picked up by Paul as a mutuality of knowledge. As the missionaries knew what happened, so do the hearers. And what the hearers remember concerns the character of the missionaries, their attitudes, their behaviour, their bearing, the strange mixture of their brave confidence, their self-effacing humility and the heavy burdens they carried for themselves and for others: *You know what we were like for your sake when we were with you* (1.5d).

This knowledge of what kind of people the missionaries were, became, within those extraordinary circumstances, a pattern to be followed, and a pattern evident in the Lord Christ (see Introduction, section 10), and indeed you became followers of *the example set by us and by the Lord* (v. 6a). The consequence of a warm and positive reception of the message was evidence of that; *the welcome you gave to the message meant grave suffering for you, yet you rejoiced in the Holy Spirit* (v. 6bc). The strange mixture of confidence and humility they had observed in the missionaries, and the burdens they carried became, they soon discovered, to be their own also. Moreover, the Holy Spirit which had marked the circumstances of receiving the message, was a mark of divine choice and vocation and a source of joy and new life. It is difficult to avoid quoting the parallel in Gal. 3.1–5: 'Jesus Christ was openly displayed on the cross! . . . How then did you receive the Spirit?' The Spirit's work among the Galatians marked the new beginning of the Gentile converts' way of life: 'When God gives you the Spirit and works miracles among you, is it because you keep the law, or is it because you have faith in the gospel message?' The picture in Galatians is of circumstances similar to those envisaged in 1 Thessalonians, even though the point which Paul is making is couched in the contrast of 'law' and 'Spirit', a contrast which never appears in the Thessalonian correspondence.

Paul's exposition of that initial entry of the missionaries into Thessalonica, together with the memories they all had of those events, is by no means complete yet: *and so you have become a model for all believers in Macedonia and in Achaia* (v. 7). That does not mean (or does not only mean) that those who had accepted the Christian faith followed now the Thessalonians' way of life. The 'model' – perhaps Paul moves to a different picture here from a 'pattern to be imitated', one more suited to the set of circumstances which he has described – the 'model' had become itself a vital form of the message which had spread like the pealing of a bell across the landscape: For *from you the word of the Lord had rung out; and not in Macedonia and Achaia alone . . .* (v. 8). The evidence for this could only have come from Paul's colleagues. As we saw earlier, the only cities in Macedonia he had visited were Philippi, Thessalonica and Beroea, and the only areas in Achaia would have been Corinth and towns and villages near Corinth. Silvanus and Timothy had the time and opportunity to visit more widely in both Macedonia and Achaia. Whether or not they did so, we cannot tell. They could have provided the information which Paul now includes. So of course could the many travellers, traders, refugees and officials with whom the missionaries came into contact. Whoever spread the information gave the impression that the news had been effective even more widely: in every place *your faith in God has become common knowledge* (there is a play on words here between 'model' and 'place').

An important change is taking place at this stage in the chapter. When Paul began to record the spread of the Thessalonians' faith, his record was in terms of the spreading of events in Thessalonica as part of the good news that had rung out. Paul's task in the letter was to convince the converts that the hope promised to them could become at the parousia of the Lord a perfected reality for them all, despite all their anxieties, fears and uncertainties about themselves and their colleagues.

A subtle change is taking place in the chapter. At this stage in the opening chapter Paul turns to what has been implied in the story so far but has not as yet been made explicit. The people who were there in Thessalonica and who witnessed the events were Gentiles. So it was not only what had happened that spread across the Mediterranean world. This was indeed 'the word of the Lord' (the message concerning the good news and how the good news had proved effective as the missionaries embodied the gospel and the divine choice of the Gentiles was realized among the Thessalonians). What also spread across the world was the news of the Gentiles' response to God's call, a response which included a new commitment to and a reshaped understanding of God (and that applied to God-fearers as much as to pagans): 'everywhere your faith in respect of God had gone out, so *no words of ours are needed*' (v. 8d). As a way of summarizing what happened in Thessalonica Paul could refer to it as *the story of our visit to you* (v. 9b); and that is an object of his thanksgiving in this chapter. It is also an important part of the pastoral response which he is shaping. Part of his response to the anxieties of the Thessalonians is what happened in Thessalonica. As Paul has built up the common, agreed understanding of what happened, he has already built into the story three features of the Thessalonians' faith which contain an important response to their anxieties. Now at this point in the chapter he makes the three features explicit; and in doing so he also enables us to see more clearly precisely where the anxieties and fears of the Thessalonian Gentiles lay.

These three elements are not intended as a total picture of the Thessalonians' faith. Alone they give rather a strange impression (Hooker-Stacey, p. 158). They are the features of the Thessalonians' faith which relate particularly to their main anxieties and fears, and which Paul intends to use in order to show how those fears can be allayed. As the Thessalonians responded to the good news in those initial and astonishing events, they had become aware of God's choice, that God had chosen Gentiles to forward the work of salvation. In so doing God revealed himself as a *true and living God* (see Introduction, section 10). Their response of faith is described by Paul in the words: *You have turned from idols to be servants of the true and living God* (v. 9).

'Turning from idols' was in itself an uprooting, a brave and demanding uprooting in so far as it removed their earlier securities, false though those may have been – brave in that it set them against the stream of local religious, social and political life; and demanding in that they moved from an understanding of religion which favoured lax and self-indulgent behaviour to faith in a God whose holiness summoned the reshaped people of God to be holy. The interaction between faith in the true and living God and the style and quality of life that such faith required is best understood initially from the background provided by Jewish documents of their time. One Jewish document of his time with which Paul was familiar and which he later used in writing the letter to the Romans was the Wisdom of Solomon. We do not know at what stage in his life he first met that material and in what form he knew it. But the Wisdom of Solomon offers a good summary of factors which Paul wove into his letters: that God is One, that his wisdom and truth founded the world, that the creation obeys his commands and enables the fulfilment of his work of salvation and judgement. He is therefore a living and active God, not bound by creation but Lord over all his works (Breytenbach, pp. 6–24). He is known as such by those whom he has called, and who therefore serve him in thankful obedience. Those who worship wood and stone (a somewhat oversimple, but nevertheless for Paul's purpose practical way of describing idolatry) find their abilities, skills, purposes and hopes atrophied, and their human desires, emotions and urges, originally intended for holy use, rendered impure. To serve the true and living God is consequently to recover in obedience to God the true fulfilment of who we are as human beings – as we might say, in body, mind and spirit. (How Paul addresses the wholeness of life we shall find out later; see the commentary on 1 Thess. 4.23.) Whether or not Paul first found such an understanding of service to the true and living God from the Wisdom of Solomon, as a background to Paul's understanding of God, it serves us well.

The anxieties involved in such a 'turning from idols' were multiple: the newness of the demands and their intensity, the memory of past patterns of life and the understanding of judgement, the awareness of being novices in a strange country, and the barely understood values of goodness, purity and holiness. Over against those anxieties and fears there stood the joy, exhilaration and wonder of discovering a new family, a people of God being reshaped by their own presence in the family as Gentiles. Their story and that of the missionaries was of discovering that they belonged to a people loved by God, so that their lives are defined by God's grace and peace. The two experiences belong together: their sense of being novices, and the overarching reality of the true and living God.

The Thessalonians' response of faith is described by Paul, secondly, as *to wait expectantly for his Son from heaven* (v. 10a). 'Hope in our Lord Jesus Christ' has already featured as the third of the Triad in Paul's account of events in Thessalonica (1.3). In 1.10 that hope points to the parousia, to the coming of the Lord from heaven, a coming which will feature in 4.16: 'when the command is given, when the archangel's voice is heard, when God's trumpet sounds, then the Lord himself will descend from heaven'. At the parousia the Thessalonians know that they can hope in Jesus Christ. But almost uniquely in Paul's letters the Jesus Christ who is to come from heaven at the Parousia is called 'God's Son' – 'to wait expectantly for his Son from heaven'. Paul speaks of God's sending of Jesus Christ as his Son so that we can through him attain sonship, given by the Son's Spirit the right to call God 'Father' (see 1.1), heirs by God's own act (Gal. 4. 4–6), ordained to share the likeness of his Son (Rom. 8.29). Our life is lived by faith in the Son of God, 'who loved me and gave himself for me' (Gal. 2.20; see 1 Thess. 5.10). Since God by an act of power raised his Son from the dead (Rom. 1.4), those who share his sonship are to share his risen life. Behind those quotations from Paul stand three important insights into 1 Thess. 1.10. First, the Son shared our death, the death of Adam, so that sharing his life we may live with him (1 Thess. 5.10). There is the hope in Christ of our restoration to the true state of humanity (see Ecclus 14.20—15.10). Second, as God's Risen Son he is Lord, seated at the right hand of God, interceding for us now and at the last judgement. Third, God's Son enables his integrity, reliability and perseverance to be reflected in those who proclaim him (Hooker-Stacey, pp. 160, 168). Hope in Jesus Christ, to which the Thessalonians have been committed since the events in Thessalonica led them to turn to God, is seen against that background and, under those three headings, is a direct response to the anxieties and fears of the Thessalonians. God, through Christ, will see them through to the fulfilment of his purposes for them.

The third response of the Thessalonians' faith, as described by Paul, is: *Jesus our deliverer from the retribution to come* (1.10c). The word translated 'retribution' (in Greek '*orge*', and often translated 'anger' or 'wrath'), is rendered in the same way by the REB in 1 Thess. 5.9: 'God has not destined us for retribution but for the full attainment of salvation through our Lord Jesus Christ'. To the modern ear 'retribution' in those contexts, sounds as if we are due to be paid back for the evil we have done or, some would say rather more precisely, as if we deserve to have inflicted on us as a consequence of an evil action that which corresponds to or is the equivalent of such an act. In both contexts then, Jesus would be ensuring that does not happen in our case. Neither of those two ideas seems altogether consonant with our moral awareness today, and neither is entirely acceptable as a guide to the nature and purpose of God. In both passages, in 1.10 and 5.9, NIV and NRSV prefer the translation 'wrath', but that translation too needs considerable explanation if it is to communicate accurately what Paul intended. 'Wrath' or 'anger' has too many associations with a destructive intent or effect. Unfortunately, it does not take the matter of a New Testament interpretation of '*orge*' much further forward if we trace Paul's use of the word back into the Greek translation of the Old Testament, and to the Hebrew words which '*orge*' translated. Divine wrath in the Old Testament corresponds in some ways to material concerning the gods in the ancient Near East: anger that seeks to destroy humankind, that intervenes in the destiny of nations, that destroys shrines and temples, and that brings individuals into deadly danger. In Israel's God, of course, as the different levels of divine action illustrate, 'anger' and 'mercy' seem to coexist in the divine nature (see Isa. 45.8: 'In an upsurge of anger I hid my face from you for a moment but now I pitied you with never-failing love, says the Lord, your Deliverer' (where 'Deliverer' translates the same Greek word as in 1 Thess. 1.10). In post-Auschwitz days language suggesting such divine interventions lacks credence and finds only limited space even in forms of modern Jewish theology.

As far as the Thessalonian correspondence is concerned there is a still more basic question to ask about '*orge*': is '*orge*' to be understood as 'God's wrath'? In none of the three uses is that clearly to be understood. There are examples in the Pauline corpus where the text reads 'God's wrath' (Rom. 1.18; Col. 3.6; Eph. 5.6); but that leaves 16 cases where '*orge*' lacks the designation 'of God'. The three examples of 'God's wrath' relate closely to depictions of atrophied humanity of the kind considered earlier in the Wisdom of Solomon, and could well express not God's retributive or judicial judgement but rather God's handing over of those who are disobedient, rebellious and untruthful to the consequences of their actions and attitudes. In the case of other examples where '*orge*' stands alone, the same could be said: those who are disobedient are left to the outworking of their own devices. In terms of 1 Thess. 5.9 there are those who are left by God to the chaos they have created and there are those who are to attain salvation through Jesus Christ. 1 Thess. 1.10 is slightly different since there the 'wrath' is described as 'the coming wrath', and Jesus as the deliverer is described by a participle which could refer to a present activity as well as to a future saviour. The events in Thessalonica have included a warning given by Paul that disaster and chaos are already at work and will result in those who distance themselves from God being left to their own catastrophic devices. The Thessalonians heeded the warning, turning from idols to serve the true and living God, waiting for his Son from heaven and acknowledging Jesus as the one who delivers and will ultimately deliver them from the disastrous consequences of a despairing and broken society, opening up for them the rich and fulfilling life with Christ to be shared with all God's people. We shall find that 1 Thess. 2.16 alludes similarly to what results from opposition to the living God. 2 Thess. 1.2–10 requires a separate discussion but in fact fits a not dissimilar pattern.

Our reading of 1 Thess. 1.2–10 is an exposition of the astonishing events in Thessalonica, of the effectiveness of a vibrant community, shaped by the Holy Spirit as testimony to all that God has done through the missionaries' activities, and the community's commitment to a way of salvation in obedience to God the Father in expectation of the coming of his Son and in recognition of Jesus' deliverance from chaos to salvation. These events concerned Gentiles who shared with the missionaries' trials and tribulations, among which were the dislocations and antipathies of their colleagues, families and neighours, and their own questioning of their worthiness for the kingdom promised them. Paul's response has been to build with them, in thankfulness to God for all that had happened, the recollections of where they began, and of the resources given them and grasped by them. Those resources are sufficient to overcome their anxieties and sense of unsuitability and unworthiness, as Paul will try to demonstrate.

There is, however, a query which might weaken the picture which they have built together. 1 Thess. 2.1–12 must address that.

The visit of Paul and Silvanus: Paul's view
2.1–12

Ch. 2 opens with a further appeal to the Thessalonians' knowledge of the missionaries' arrival, the first of four such appeals: For *you know . . . yourselves, my friends, that our visit to you was not fruitless* (2.1). That is the first appeal; there will be an awakening of their memory of the missionaries' work (2.9) a crucial appeal to the Thessalonians and to God as witnesses (2.10). and an appeal to what the Thessalonians remember of the missionaries' style of life (2.11), All four are appeals regarding the character of 'the Thessalonica event'. The vocabulary of 'what happened', begun in 1.2–10, is continued into 2.1, 7, 8, 10. The shared knowledge of what happened is the basis for what Paul is about to say next (see the opening word 'For'). It is important for Paul that the events were not 'in vain'.

There is however an important shift of emphasis. Whereas hitherto 'the visit' has tended to include '*all* that happened', here Paul is particularly concerned with the part which he and Silvanus played in those events, and that what they did was not 'in vain'. The REB uses the word 'fruitless' in 2.1. In Phil. 2.16 the translation used is 'in vain'; there Paul pleads with the Philippians to show innocent and faultless behaviour that will confirm Paul's labour as not 'in vain'. 'In vain' has strong Old Testament prophetic resonances. It is never easy to be sure that Paul has Old Testament patterns in mind, unless he specifically quotes from Scripture. But there are passages in the Greek text of Isaiah which have clear resonances with 1 Thess. 2.1 (and with Phil. 2.16). In Isa. 49.1–6 God's servant, uncertain if his work is in vain, commits the results of his labour to God's judgement, and is given the task of bearing the news of God's salvation. In Isa. 65.23 the work of God's chosen one is promised the fruition of God's blessing. 'In vain' can imply both 'ineffective' and 'fruitless'; and it is quite possible that in 1 Thess. 2.1 Paul had in mind both the fruitfulness of their labours and the effectiveness of their arrival. But if he did, then he was clear that the power that became evident in those events (see 1.5 and the commentary there) was divine. 1 Thess. 2 points, as we shall see, in that direction too. So translation of 2.1 could read either 'not fruitless' or 'not powerless'. Paul has chosen a phrase which could mean either or both; he probably meant both. But the emphasis has shifted from the wider picture of 'the visit' to the narrower issue of what the missionaries did, and that it was not 'in vain'.

Far from it! (2.2) he exclaims; the visit was far from fruitless and powerless, and the missionaries' work shows that. The central action of the verse is 'we began to *declare the gospel of God to you frankly and fearlessly*', either 'in the strength of God' or 'within God's plan and purpose'. The action centres on the missionaries' work. According to the verse's final phrase their work was, *in the face of great opposition* (that is, the difficulties were caused by external forces). Equally possible is a different translation 'in the midst of a great struggle'(Malherbe, p. 137 – the Greek word here is *'agon'* the word for 'contest'), which certainly could include external problems, but would involve a host of other difficulties too: financial (how did they afford initial food and shelter), emotional (they had not emerged from Philippi unscathed), physical (what state was Paul in?) and psychological (teaching made enormous demands on their inner resources). In these respects, when Paul speaks of 'a great struggle', he was making a point vital to his argument. He saw the missionaries' work not in terms of personal success or failure, nor in terms of personal survival; he was reshaping the 'agonistic' culture of the world around him, where every social interaction was 'agonistic', a matter of competition, power and honour. Through God's grace the missionaries fulfilled their task

21

but 'in the midst of great struggle'. The position of that phrase at the very end of the verse draws attention to what we read at its beginning: *After all the injury and outrage which as you know we had suffered in Philippi*. The effect of the REB's translation 'After all the injury and insult' in Philippi we began to 'declare the gospel of God to you frankly and fearlessly in the face of great opposition' gives the impression of a major contrast between what the missionaries did in Philippi and what they did in Thessalonica. The opening of 2.2 creates a major contrast between the experiences of Philippi and the freedom of speech in Thessalonica. Although that is possible, if the final phrase of 2.2 is translated 'in the midst of a great struggle' the contrast with the insults and outrage in Philippi begins to disappear. Indeed because of the limited time lapse between the departure from Philippi and entry into Thessalonica the two experiences begin to coalesce: We missionaries suffered, as you know, injury and outrage in Philippi, and we began to preach fearlessly 'in the midst of a great struggle' in Thessalonica too.

Our knowledge of the end of the Philippian stay is mainly culled from Acts in its various recensions (Barrett, pp. 783–805). Destruction of local business profits, mistaken identities, mob pressure, laws on foreign cults, charging, beating, imprisoning of innocent victims, fear of contiuing aggression, magistrates anxious that the trouble-makers should depart – all these are part of the experience to which Paul was alluding. Since the Thessalonians knew the facts about events in Philippi, the atmosphere surrounding the missionaries' arrival could well have been one of suspicion, especially since, although the facts were known, the motivations of the missionaries were not. Perhaps 1 Thess. 2.2 is saying that the arrival was certainly not in vain because of the divinely inspired and fearless initial proclamation, yet neither before nor during their initial work were the circumstances easy. The pressures before and during were hardly sustainable physically and mentally. Of the local furore in Philippi the Thessalonians were only too aware; and, according to Acts, it was not long before the same troubles erupted in Thessalonica. In brief, according to 1 Thess. 2.1–2, the missionaries came with a reputation, and one which would not easily be lived down. Nevertheless, as both Paul and the Thessalonians recognized, God was at work and so their labours were not in vain.

The character of the missionaries was crucial to the picture which Paul and the Thessalonians had built together in thankfulness to God (1.5c). Any queries against their good name would be fatal to the final outcomes from their visit. Paul must try to anticipate any problems that might threaten to undermine the event they had shared. That is what he does in the following passage. In an argument which resembles that of the Old Testament prophets (and Paul elsewhere alludes to that similarity: Gal. 1.15) Paul seeks from the Thessalonians the testimony that the missionaries have worked with divine authorization and qualification (see Jer. 1.5 and, again, Isa. 49.1–6).

Three consequences flow from the claim to divine authorization and qualification: *the appeal we make does not spring from delusion or sordid motive or from any attempt to deceive* (2.3). The background and translation of the three words translated here 'delusion', 'sordid motive' and 'attempt to deceive' have been discussed in relation to philosophical, biblical and moral traditions. Certainly it is also possible to understand the three terms as illustrations of 'seeking to please human beings' – *currying favour with men* – rather than God (see 2.4b). But the context requires Paul's argumentation to be based on divine authorization. The appeal he makes for confirmation springs from the true and living God. So, for example, 'error' (perhaps a better translation than 'delusion'; Wanamaker, p. 94) has no place in their work. That is the word's translation in the Wisdom of Solomon 12.14. 'They had strayed far down the paths of error, taking for gods the most despised and hideous creatures.' The missionaries have not led the Thessalonians into error; they have led them from the ways of error to know and serve the true and living God. Their appeal cannot have sprung from error. The God known through the Holy Spirit summons all to holiness; the missionaries' appeal therefore cannot have sprung from the opposite of holiness, that is, impurity (see the use of '*akatharsia*', 'impurity' in 1 Thess. 4.7, but translated here in the REB as 'sordid motive'). Holiness precludes 'deceit' too; 'deceit' is a feature of idol-worship (see Wisdom 14.30, where vows before idols make a mockery of holiness). All these three – error, impurity, deceit – cannot belong to those named fit by the true God to proclaim the gospel. Paul's defence is theological rather than philosophical.

There is one example from the Pauline letters where Paul has to defend himself from the charge of 'deceit': 2 Cor. 12.16. But that charge derived from the Collection for the Saints, well after the Thessalonian letters were written; the charge in that case was answered in terms of the integrity of those involved in the collection. In 1 Thess. 2.3–4 there is no reason here to assume that any of the three, error, impurity or deceit, relates to direct charges made against Paul. 1 Thess. 2 is not an apology in that sense. Paul was arguing from God's authorization to what is to be expected of a missionary and from what he and his colleagues fulfil.

In 2.5–8 Paul returns to the events in Thessalonica, and the kind of people the missionaries have turned out to be (1.5c). Paul admits that as *Christ's envoys* (or, apostles) *'we could have made our weight felt'*, but he reminds the Thessalonians that in fact they became *gentle among you . . . As a nurse caring for her children*. This is not the only place in the Pauline letters where Paul admits that as apostles they enjoy certain privileges and could have made their status felt. In 1 Cor. 9 he lists privileges he might have chosen to claim:

> Have I not right to take a Christian wife about with me, like the rest of the apostles and the Lord's brothers and Cephas? Are only Barnabas and I bound to work for our living? Did you ever hear of a man serving in the army at his own expense? . . . My case does not rest on these human analogies, . . . in the law of Moses we read, 'You shall not muzzle an ox while it is treading out the grain.'

But, continues Paul, 'I have never availed myself of any such right. On the contrary, I put up with all that comes my way rather than offer any hindrance to the gospel of Christ.' 'I am free and own no master', he adds; 'but I have made myself everyone's servant, to win over as many as possible' (1 Cor. 9.5–7a, 8, 12bc, 19). The implication in 1 Cor. 9 is that Paul is unwilling to be a financial drain on the congregation; and that is, as we shall see, relevant to the context of 1 Thess. 2.7 too. In 1 Thess. 2.9 Paul will make a point similar to that in 2.7a: 'You remember . . . our toil and drudgery; night and day we worked for a living, rather than be a burden to any of you while we proclaimed to you the good news of God' (2.9). In an example of his pastoral counselling in 1 Corinthians, Paul takes care not to use language which is too 'heavyweight' (2 Cor. 2.5 – the Greek word for 'heavyweight' is the same word Paul uses in 1 Thess. 2.9 and in 2 Thess. 3.8). In one respect the metaphor which he uses of himself and his colleagues in 1 Thess. 2.7c is relevant to the case of pastoral work: he uses the metaphor of a 'nurse caring for her very own children'. But the exact way in which Paul is using the metaphor of the nurse depends on two problems. First, a problem of the text. As the REB translation indicates, the metaphor is clearest if immediately before the metaphor the text says: *we* (plural) became (the 'happening' word again) . . . *gentle with you*. This is one example where the less well-attested reading (that is, the reading which when judged by the history of textual variations has the weaker case) may well be what Paul originally dictated. The better-attested reading is 'we were <u>children</u> with you', but that adds just one too many metaphors into the text. (Only one initial letter in the Greek distinguished 'children' from 'gentle'.) The second problem is partly of translation and partly of punctuation. The REB treats the opening word of 2.8 as adverbial and denoting measure or degree: *'Our affection was so deep'*. But that goes against Pauline and indeed general Greek usage (Fee, p. 178); it would be much closer to Pauline usage to use 'so' as a correlative to the 'as'. That offers excellent sense if a full stop is read after 'gentle with you'. (The earliest manuscripts, in the main, lack most indications of punctuation.) We prefer, then, the following translation: 'But we were gentle with you. As a nurse cares for her very own children, so we, . . . in deep affection (or 'yearning') for you, are *determined to share with you not only the gospel of God but our very selves*; for it is very *dear* indeed that *you had become* (the 'happening' word again) *to us*. The metaphor of the nurse relates both to what happened in Thessalonica and to the missionaries' continuing affection. Like a nurse who remains deeply committed to her own, the missionaries were then, and are now, willing to share their very lives (the Greek word *'psuche'*) with those in their care.

The metaphor of the nurse has been illuminated by many different commentators. Some regard the background as philosophical (Malherbe, p. 146) and quote Plutarch's *On How to Tell a Flatterer from a Friend*: 'When children fall down, the nurses do not rush up to berate them, but they take them up, wash them, and straighten their clothes, and, after all this is done, then rebuke and punish them.' But the application of the metaphor to philosophical teachers is not well attested. Some scholars stress the warm, emotional and protective aspects of the nurse's work, quoting the many tributes on Roman funerary inscriptions, an emphasis which suits well Paul's choice of language: 'the nurse tenderly cherishes her own'. Some scholars point out that this tender care provides an excellent background to Paul's argument, since such love doubles for maternal care given from love, whereas care for other people's children would usually be on the basis of paid employment. Paul's work belongs to the former not to the latter. Various aspects of spirituality have also been identified in the metaphor, whether drawn from Jewish sources or from the mystery religions (Donfried, 1985, pp. 316–56). Very important is Paul's assertion that, like the nurse, the missionaries were ready not only to share the good news but to embody that care in their own lives. That is by no means foreign to the ancient views of a nurse. One of the most famous nurses in Greek drama is Phaedra's nurse. In one of Euripides' plays she says: 'It's a heavy weight that one person should bear for two, as I feel pain for her' (*Hippolytus*, pp. 259–60). Unhappily, according to the story in the versions of both Euripides and Seneca, that deep love finds tragic expression. Paul's sacrificial love seeks a happier outcome. As far as mystery religions are concerned Paul's sacrificial love is also to be distinguished from anything to be found there; Paul's love follows the work of Christ, whose perseverance led to his death and only so to his resurrection and glorification (Wedderburn, 1987, pp. 296–359).

On the basis of Paul's appeal to the Thessalonians he can say: For *we have never resorted* [again the 'happening' word] *to flattery, as you have cause to know* (2.5a). The missionaries had refused to curry favour with people (2.4c). They had shown personal commitment to the divinely given task of preaching the gospel (2.5b). So there can be no subtle, false and cunning presentation (see 2 Cor. 4.2). Their concern was with cherishing, not fawning over the Thessalonians. *Nor as God is our witness, have our words ever been a cloak for greed* (2.5b). On the question of finance in Thessalonica Paul is, as we have already seen, in the clear (2.9); he can appeal to the source of the events in Thessalonica, to God himself. God knows their inner motives and intentions. Paul has recalled the evidence from the Thessalonians that he and his colleagues have not stood on their rights; they have not been heavy-handed; and, most important of all, they have refused to follow the rules of competition according to which you can win respect only at cost to others: *We have never sought honour.* That is not the way that love works (1.3; see 1 Cor. 13.4–7).

The character of the missionaries is crucial to the picture which Paul and the Thessalonians built in thankfulness to God for 'the Thessalonica event' (1.5c). In 1 Thess. 2 their divine authorization and their gentleness are part of what made the event possible; they illuminate the reality of the missionaries' presence in Thessalonica. That means that the chapter probably has two functions. In so far as the disturbances in Philippi, Thessalonica and Beroea aroused suspicions, in so far as unfair rumours were spread and fostered, in so far as separation from the Thessalonians gave rise to anxiety, and in so far as there were attempts to weaken the apostles' hold on the congregation by unknown Christians, by Jews or by townsfolk, the opening verses, built on the Thessalonians' own evidence, provided a safeguard for the converts' confidence in what happened when the missionaries first arrived. In 2.9–12 a second function is beginning to appear. An important fact in 1.6 had been that the Thessalonians had begun to imitate the missionaries and their Lord. The imitation was highly successful, and became a well-known and powerful testimony to what had happened in Thessalonica. For Gentiles the change, as Paul described it 1.9–10, was massive and disruptive. It was a call to a new and strange pattern of life, one which would need (as Paul will remind them later) gifts of discernment. What more important task could Paul perform than to clarify what imitation involved. 2.1–12 will make a contribution to that goal. What Paul may not have realized was the extent to which this call for the missionaries to be imitated would appear arrogant.

The shape of 2.9–12 is somewhat different from 2.3–4 and 2.5–8, although like those passages (and like 1.3) they abound in triads; and like 2.5–8 Paul uses a metaphor as a focus. 2.9–12 begins with the reminder of the missionaries' hard work to earn a living *rather than be a burden to any of you while we proclaimed to you the good news of God*. What kind of pattern for imitation did that provide? Paul draws the moral inference in 4.11–12: 'Work with your hands, as we told you, so that you may command the respect of those outside your own number, and at the same time never be in want.' This is an artisan pattern (Murphy O'Connor, p. 117), and leaves the impression that what happened in Thessalonica involved a group who had to work in company with others to have sufficient to live on.

The first triad reads like a summary of the chapter so far: this is the way the missionaries lived, and they offer it as a pattern to follow. *We call you to witness, yes and God himself, how devout and just and blameless was our conduct* [the 'happening word again] *towards you who are believers* (v. 10). 'Devout' aptly summarizes 2.3–4; it designates a way of life pleasing to God, consecrated by and to God, the Holy One; 'just' picks up elements of 3.5–8, especially the avoidance of greed and greediness, of competition at the cost of others, of standing by one's own rights irrespective of the needs of others and of the work of God; 'blameless' is a more challenging word, as the prayer in 3.13 reveals. That is God's ultimate project; it begins in the process of confirmation, continues in the search for holiness, and finds its fulfilment before God at the parousia, alongside all the saints. If that seems – and it must have seemed so to some Gentile converts – to be an unrealistic project, then at least Paul's list of negative implications of holy and righteous living demonstrated toward them and witnessed by them, would have made 'blameless' living seem at least feasible. God's ultimate project was daunting. It remains so in the light of the complexities we noted in section 1 of the Introduction. To attend to Paul's responses to the Thessalonians is to recognize that they needed to be theological then, as responses to the world's anxieties still do today.

2.9–13 contains a central metaphor, as does 2.5–8. The metaphor in 2.9–13 is that of the *father* dealing *with each* of his children individually. The Thessalonians have noted that this is how Paul worked. Whereas the pattern of the nurse's work is valued particularly for offering loving commitment, the father's is valued for personal exhorting, encouraging and testifying for each member of the household. The missionaries have, like the nurse, offered themselves in loving service, and, like a father, they have given personal guidance to help the Thessalonians to live *lives worthy of the God who calls* them. The Thessalonians have observed how they worked and can testify to its effectiveness. The interesting question arises whether Paul regards these sections not only as confirmation of what happened initially in Thessalonica, but also as guidance for imitation (Marguerat, pp. 25–34). In one sense that is hardly possible for the Thessalonians. The apostles occupied in those events in Thessalonica a position which no one else could have. They gave an initiatory example of service and teaching. On the other hand, most certainly some aspects of the nurse's and the father's responsibilities are there to be imitated. In 1 Thess. 5.14 some of the father's tasks are to be exercised within the community: the idle are to be rebuked, the faint-hearted encouraged and the weak supported. The care and guidance are to be adjusted personally to individual needs. The Thessalonians will also be expected to make responsible, discrimating (in the best sense) judgements (5.21a). Certainly they must exercise care for each other. It is quite justified to conclude that 1 Thess. 2 is both confirmation of the integrity of what happened in Thessalonica and a model to be followed. *We appealed to you, we encouraged you, we urged you, to live lives worthy of the God who calls you into his kingdom and glory* (2.12).

Paul ends the section with this reminder that the ultimate project is indeed ultimate. There is much discussion of what Paul means by the 'kingdom'. Often in Paul the kingdom is spoken of as a future inheritance (1 Cor. 6.9–10; Gal. 5.21). It is a glorious inheritance, as is also implied in 1 Cor. 15.50, and one which, it is intended, the Thessalonians will be worthy to enter (1 Thess. 2.12; 2 Thess. 1.5). It is a future inheritance. It is also in one particular sense a present reality. It is a present reality in the sense found in the First Ode in the Septuagint. Speaking of God's people the psalmist prays there that God will lead them in and plant them upon the mountain of his inheritance, the holy sanctuary 'which your hands prepared – the lord ruling age by age and onward'. The kingdom is present because it is eternal. Such an idea recalls the 'heavenly Jerusalem' of Gal. 4.26, and provides an ultimate destination for the people of God in 1 Thess. 4.13–18. Just as the kingdom in that sense is both future and present, so to be worthy to enter the kingdom requires a pattern of living which is appropriate both to the present and to what is to come. Often Paul's theology is summarized as a 'now but not yet'. According to the above pattern of understanding the kingdom, the 'now but not yet' is not quite exact. What God in Christ offers is 'now and still to come'.

The second thanksgiving
2.13

A fresh thanksgiving introduces the next section (2.14–16), and the thanksgiving is closely linked with Paul's argument so far. 'And this is in fact why' *we thank God continually* (Moule, p. 161). The following phrase confirms our reading of Paul's argument so far. The reason for thankfulness is now repeated in summary form, preparing the way for the next step which Paul initiates (some might call this a 'peroratio'; he recapitulates his main theme): *when we handed on God's message, you accepted it, not as the word of men, but as what it truly is, the very word of God at work in you who are believers*. The REB translation here picks up the detail of this dense summary. 'Handed on' places the missionaries and the Thessalonians in the line of a tradition which has to be passed on. 1 Cor. 15.1 makes the same point using the same term: 'the gospel that I preached; the gospel which you received'. 'God's message' is literally 'the report from us, which is God's'. We are accustomed to this use of the word 'report' (see Isa. 53.1 and Rom. 10.10). It is the prophetic proclamation which goes out with divine authority and power – and so, God's message delivered and received in the mutuality described in 1 Thess. 1.6–7. 'Not as the words of men' recalls that the gospel was not in word only but also 'in power, namely with the Holy Spirit and full conviction'. What happened in Thessalonica was no human enterprise; 'the Thessalonica event' was the work of God. 'At work in you who believe' draws together all the consequences which grew from that event, including the 'ringing out' of the word of God as a testimony to everything that had happened in and through the Thessalonians, and, appropriately enough at the end of this section, not least through imitation of the missionaries.

The example of the churches
2.14–16

There is one particular feature of 1 Thess. 1.2–10 of which this pithy summary makes no mention; and that is because it is to initiate Paul's next step. The Thessalonians, too, received the word 'in grave suffering'. In this respect also they 'followed the example set' by the missionaries 'and by the Lord' (1.6). Since that initial entry of the missionaries in Thessalonica much had happened and the reception of the gospel 'in grave suffering' had led to the local difficulties and trials. These Paul interprets as further illustrations of Thessalonian 'imitation': For *you have followed the example* of Christians elsewhere; literally 'For you have become [the 'happening' word again] imitators' of Christians elsewhere. The Thessalonians had previously followed the example of the missionaries and the Lord; more recently they have also *followed the example of the Christians in the churches in Judaea* (2.14). Paul has in mind the trouble caused by the townsfolk in Thessalonica, and he sets these troubles alongside what the Judaean Christians suffered at the hands of local people (either at the initial stages of the preaching of the good news, or more recently; see Introduction, section 6): *you* in your turn *have been treated by your own countrymen as they* [the Judaean churches] *were treated by the* Judaeans. For Paul 'imitation' is no isolated phenomenon; 'imitation' is a sequence going back to Christ's perseverance and death. It is therefore a privilege of the highest order, a privilege such as the earliest Christians experienced, in many respects an unwanted privilege. It was not one either to seek or to evade. That is his interpretation of the Thessalonian experiences at the hands of their townsfolk. In offering it Paul is also aware of another factor, one which causes him personally great anguish (it is an *'agon'* in the double sense of a challenge and a personal agony). Jews – and Paul could not forget that he was a Jew (1 Cor. 9.20) – were responsible (or perhaps according to Paul 'a particular group' of the Jews were responsible – see below – but even this modified viewpoint causes discomfort in a post-Auschwitz age) for the death of the Jesus, as they were for the death of the prophets. It is understandable that Paul, having begun with the Thessalonians' trials, should have wished to continue the line of 'imitation' back to the Lord himself. The Thessalonians are imitators of him, and he is the paradigm of perseverance in the extremities of suffering. But why should he have continued the story back before Jesus? That is a different question. The charge that they killed the prophets needs an explanation.

It has a long history, notably back in the Deuteronomic tradition and then forward into the Gospel tradition (see Matt. 23.29–32). The same subject also appears in another Pauline comment, albeit in a different form. On the killing of the prophets in Rom. 11.3–4 he quotes the story of Elijah complaining to God that he alone is left and they wish to kill him too (1 Kgs 19.9b–14). There Paul is underlining the hopeful side of Israel's story, that a righteous remnant has constantly remained despite the killing of God's messengers. In 1 Thess. 2.14–15 Paul's use of the 'killing of the prophets' tradition is rather different. In 1 Thess. 2.14–15 he links the killing of the prophets with the killing of Jesus (probably, according to Paul by a specific group of Jews; the comma after 'the Jews' at the end of 2.14 in the REB is probably incorrect). Paul further links those traditions with the fact that Jews (again specific groups of Jews) have caused the missionaries to be driven out. In this 'they (the Jews) do not please God' (see 2.14; 4.1) and are opposed to all humankind in that *they hinder us from telling the Gentiles how they may be saved* (2.15–16a). Paul is building up an extended list of examples of Jewish disobedience to God, stretching back into Old Testament times and forward to his (Paul's) own day, when Jews caused Paul and Silvanus to be driven out of Thessalonica and then subsequently from Beroea (Acts 17.5–10). God had called the Gentiles to be saved, as the gift of the Holy Spirit proved; so in doing what they did the Jews were acting in disobedience to God.

The next phrase has caused much ink to be spilt: 'so as always to fill *up the measure of their* sins'. The most likely meaning of the phrase is that, as the generations have been going by, from the prophets, through the time of Jesus to that of the missionaries, in each generation the sins of disobedience mounted up toward their limit. This makes good sense of the word which means 'always', and the tense of the infinitive which could have been continuous but is probably deliberately not: 'Always, generation by generation, they took their sins to the limit.' The final phrase depends for its meaning on the word *'orge'*, 'wrath': *But* then *'wrath' overtook them* finally (2.16d). In the earlier discussion of 'wrath' we noted that the REB translation of *'orge'* in 1.10 was probably misleading; *'orge'* does not mean retribution. We saw that 'orge' has many meanings and contexts in the Old Testament, and that in Paul 'orge' explores the atrophied experiences of humanity where humanity has been disobedient to God. It marks out disaster and chaos as a consequence of such disobedience, and sees 'wrath' in this sense leading to a state where people are left to their own devices. In 1 Thess. 1.10, where Jesus' redemptive work is being described, it is likely that such a state belongs to the parousia. That is by no means necessarily the case here or in every Pauline context. According to Paul in 1 Thess. 2.15–16 Jews, by no means necessarily all Jews, have always been near the limit. Now, with the opposition to God's purpose of salvation to the Gentiles, the Jews who have hindered God's work of mission to the Gentiles have gone over the limit. They are left to their own devices. 'Wrath' in that sense and at that moment, presumably the moment when they had the missionaries expelled, had overtaken them, at last.

There are four further comments to make on this difficult section of 1 Thessalonians. First, one of the problems in 2.16 has been the assumption that, according to Paul, what has overtaken Jews is God's final judgement. We can see from the above discussion that, as in 1.10, 'wrath' is not in 2.16 about God's final judgement. Paul's thought is more subtle than that.

Second, a further problem in 2.16. On the grounds of previous translations, it has been argued, 2.16 could not be reconciled with Paul's discussion of the future of the Jewish people in Romans 9—11. If God's final judgement had fallen on Israel, then the conclusion in Rom. 11.25–29 would be impossible. If, however, 2.16

refers to the groups of Jews who overstepped the limit on disobedience by expelling the missionaries, then the tension between 1 Thessalonians 2 and Romans 9—11 is by no means irreconcilable. There is even room within the Thessalonian pattern for a righteous remnant. Paul in 1 Thessalonians is dealing with a moment at which he has seen Jews crossing their Rubicon. They have taken a step which they cannot retrace. They have hindered the preaching of the gospel to Gentiles, a violent act of disobedience to God. But Israel's fate is not thereby sealed. 1 Thess. 2.16 and Rom. 11.25–29 are at one on the really crucial matters; a final judgement has not been made on Israel; both 1 Thessalonians and Romans recognize that 'wrath' is a handing over of human beings to their desires and passions, which constantly narrow human possibilities and options (Introduction, section 1). In this way God brings home to humanity its creatureliness (Dunn, p. 696). Moreover, 2 Thess. 2.11–12 confirms within the Thessalonian correspondence what Romans sets out in 9.18–23, that God hardens the hearts of some, but this is in order that all shall recognize their need of grace.

Third, many have doubted the authenticity of 2.13–16, or at the very least the inauthenticity of 1 Thess. 2.16 (in whole or in part). Doubts were raised on many grounds, all of which we have already seen to be weak: 2.13 was thought to be an unnecessary resumption of the thanksgiving motif; 2.16 found no resonance in 2 Thessalonians; 'imitation' was assumed to be an un-Pauline idea; 1 Thess. 2.16 and Rom. 9—11 were deemed irreconcilable; 2.16 was thought to require a memorable Jewish catastrophe such as the Fall of Jerusalem (long after Paul's time), or a persecution prior to the Thessalonian problems (see Introduction, section 6); the ferocious implications of previous translations of 1 Thess. 2.16 were judged inappropriate in a Pauline letter. With the interpretation of 2.13–15 and the more exact translation of 2.16 which we have suggested the case for inauthenticity falls.

Fourth, this is one of the several New Testament passages which in recent years has been regarded as encouraging antisemitism. With the proper susceptibilities involved in the post-Holocaust period, such concerns are inevitable. We may weaken the impact of some of Paul's statements by arguing that it was the Romans who crucified Jesus rather than his own people and that Paul himself was referring to certain Jews who were involved in Jesus' death. We can question the constant (and, as we have seen, sometimes incorrect) use of the term 'the Jews'. But western history will not allow us to escape by alleging mistakes of exegesis and translation. Paul himself would have disowned at least some of the implications read off from his text; but that again is a way of evading our current responsibilities. The world has moved on, and the Thessalonian correspondence offers many reminders that relationships between races and peoples have always needed greater care and deeper understanding than humanity has summoned to the task.

The visit of Timothy: Paul's view
2.17 — 3.10

Paul has been trying to ensure that the remarkable quality of what happened when they visited Thessalonica was not in any way undermined. Both those who brought the good news and those who received it were engaged in a divinely inspired event. The missionaries may have raised questions about their behaviour by constantly attracting the attention of troublemakers backed by Jewish opponents; their hurried departures and disappearance would not have helped the confidence of their converts. On the other hand there could have been no doubt concerning the behaviour of the missionaries when they were in Thessalonica. They were models for the Thessalonians to follow, including, as Paul foresaw, models to follow when opposition created a parallel situation to that of the Judaean churches in trouble from their local townsfolk.

The thought of what happened to the Judaean churches triggered in Paul's mind the conclusion that Jewish opposition to the Gentile mission constituted a catastrophic act of disobedience, marking a new stage in God's dealing with his ancient people. Now, in harmony with the tenor of his letter so far, with its strong emphasis on mutuality, Paul, having considered the imitation evident in the work of the Thessalonians, turns again to the missionaries' part in the story: 'Now as for us, *my friends, when for a short spell* we were orphaned and separated from you' (2.17). The REB translation – *you were lost to us* – is a powerful evocation of the picture-language used by Paul here. 'Lost to us' calls up the situation which so many families have experienced during wartime in many parts of the world: children become, if only temporarily, orphans; parents lose contact with their families with all the anguish, uncertainty and terror that produces. The family relations, which Paul had built on in order to assist Gentile converts, had received, with the missionaries' sudden departures, a severe jolt. That had been serious for the Thessalonians. For Paul and his colleagues, what happened was for them distressing, too, to a degree which is evident in the language of the following verses. They were parted from friends, and, in a sense, as well, from children who had just begun to share their parents' faith. Temporary though the separation should be – that it should be only temporary is Paul's immediate concern – it had been a severe jolt for for both parties. The maintaining of the relationships was vital. 1 Thessalonians, written in a friendly mode, was designed to serve this purpose, and Paul makes the point that the Thessalonians may be *out of sight but* certainly *not out of mind* (2.17a). The Greek text of v. 17c is slightly ambiguous: is Paul saying that the separation had made him all the more *anxious* to see them again, because the separation had been sudden and he realized an early return would be essential? Or, is he saying, in line with the REB translation of 2.17c, *we were exceedingly anxious* and greatly desirous that we might *see you again* face to face? As we have already seen, the emotional language of these verses is so strong that the second alternative seems preferable. The tone of affection in the passage is quite different from the passage in 2 Cor. 13 which also deals with the question of visits and which uses similar expressions to those of 1 Thess. 2.17–19 and 5.23–29. The warmth of the relationships here is a clue to the nature and purpose of the whole letter. It was because of this deep desire that *we* had *made up our minds to visit you* (2.18a). This is a moment in the correspondence when Paul's own personal investment in the relationship breaks through – *I Paul, more than once* (or 'on more than one occasion'; see also 3.5). What follows could mean *but Satan thwarted us*; or, 'and, it has to be put on the record along with the later actions we took, Satan hindered us'. 'Satan' is a Greek transliteration of the Hebrew word *'satan'*, the one who accuses in the council of God, just one of the many names given in the intertestamental period to the arch-enemy of God. Technically, the name should be translated 'the Satan', to stress his various functions. In the Thessalonian epistles 'the Satan' hinders Paul's work, as here, and is a personal power at work in the world (see 2 Thess. 2.7–9 and the commentary on those verses), deceiving and misleading; but eventually he is to be deprived of his power (see also Rom. 16.20). The precise circumstances which caused Paul to abort his plans are hidden within the supernatural designation – 'the Satan'.

What follows suggests that 'the Satan' is seen at work in 3.5

35

as the tempter, since the tempter there could threaten the effectiveness and fruitfulness of Paul's mission. For the thought in 2.19 moves beyond the deep affection Paul has expressed and envisages the goal he has in mind. His determination to reach the Thessalonians by some means or other has as its motivation not just personal affection, important though that may be, but also in the ultimate effectiveness and fruitfulness of the mission – of his mission, and that of his colleagues. Success in human terms is for Paul irrelevant; but work well done in the name of Christ carries its reward. Work in his name is based upon his redemptive work, just as he is also the final deliverer (1.10). Work in the name of Christ also carries with it responsibilities and these will be evident at the final judgement; and reward for their proper fulfilment will follow. 1 Cor. 3.14–15 expounds this and uses the metaphor of a building: 'If anyone's building survives [in the last judgement], he will be rewarded; if it burns down, he will have to bear the loss; yet he will escape with his life, though only by passing through the fire.' So in 2.19 Paul's mind moves to the issue of the fruitfulness of his labour and its reward, *for what hope or joy or triumphal crown is there for us when we stand before our Lord Jesus at his coming? What indeed but you?* Not only does the Thessalonians' future depend on the mission being effective; Paul and his colleagues will stand before the Lord at his parousia to answer for their work.

Although we have used the term 'parousia' several times already, this is the first actual appearance of the term in Christian literature (see 3.13; 4.15; 5.23; 2 Thess. 2.1, 8, 9; 1 Cor. 15.23). In 1 Thessalonians it is clearly the return of God's resurrected Son from heaven (1.9–10), when God will initiate the coming together of all who belong to Christ (4.14; 2 Thess. 2.1), and as the goal for which all the Lord's people are to be kept blameless (5.23). In 2 Thessalonians the revelation of the Lord is accompanied with angels and flaming fire, when he comes to be 'glorified among his saints and to be wondered at among all who have believed'. Stages in the use of 'parousia' before Paul are a matter for conjecture; they may include aspects of messianic development, of Septuagintal passages such as those from Daniel, and the use of the word 'parousia' of God's personal intervention (as in Josephus, *Antiquities* 9.50 where Elisha prays that God will reveal his power and parousia (= presence) to give the prophet hope and courage). We may not know its early Christian origins but by the end of the New Testament period it had become a feature of Christian writings. Some suggest that the 'parousia' became a model in the Thessalonian letters for the apostolic arrival too, but the evidence offered for this lacks any clear shape.

At the Lord's parousia the Thessalonians will be Paul's 'hope', 'joy' and 'triumphal crown'. 'Hope' here designates the confidence before the Lord which the Thessalonian fruitfulness will promise for the apostles at the future parousia of the Lord. It is parallel to Paul's use of 'the very seal of my apostleship' in 1 Cor. 9.2. 'Joy' characterized the happenings in Thessalonica and reveals the nature of the Lord's parousia as the apostles will know it. 'The triumphal crown', literally a 'crown of boasting' underlines the justifiable pride of the apostles as their extended work with the Thessalonians reaches its final climax. The phrase reflects Old Testament and intertestamental usage (see Ezek. 16.12), but in Paul it parallels the triumphal wreath which never fades (1 Cor. 9.25). Achievement at the athletic agon/contest is marked by a fading wreath; this agon is marked by an unfading wreath, as long as, of course, no disqualification occurs (1 Cor. 9.27). As we have seen, a feature of 2 Thessalonians is the shared glory at the Lord's parousia. As humanity is returned through the work of God in Christ to its original state, 'being in the image of God's glory' is a feature of that return: 'so that the name of our Lord Jesus may be glorified in you, and you in him' (2 Thess. 1.12). It is the ultimate in apostolic achievement to have enabled that restoration to be realized. So, of the Thessalonians Paul can say: *You are our glory and our joy.*

The possibility of failure remained. Despite all the efforts of the apostolic missionaries, despite the astonishing happenings in Thessalonica when they first arrived, 'the labour might still be wasted' (3.5d). Had their time been wasted? Paul's narration in 1 Thess. 3.1–10 begins with the sending of Timothy to Thessalonica to assess what was happening there and it concludes with his return, bringing reassuring news and for Paul thankful delight. 'The Satan' or 'the tempter' did not have the last word. There had come a point when having been hindered, Paul could not stand the tensions of the situation any longer. The language of 'being orphaned' (2.17) has its echo in 3.1: *So when we could bear it no longer, we* [in this context 'we' means 'I'] *decided to stay on alone at Athens.* In Introduction, section 3 we worked out roughly how Paul came to be in Athens, without Silvanus, so that sending Timothy meant that he was left alone. But 1 Thess. 3.1–5 is a powerful narration that has been pared down to its essentials; we have seen the pressure continuing to build (2.17–20); the dam has to burst; the decision is made gladly, it means being abandoned – to endure desolation and anxiety in Athens. The narration has intentional pathos. The Thessalonians need to know what Paul went through and why. Other details are unimportant. *We* [again = 'I'; see 3.5] *sent Timothy*. The commendation of Timothy seems surprisingly brief. But, by the time Paul was writing, Timothy needed no introduction; for better or worse his task was done. Thankfully he had done well. So a few bold claims suffice: *our colleague* [or, brother], *a co-worker with God* [brief, but certainly bold; see the commentary on 2.3–4, especially when expanded by the phrase which follows] *in the service of the gospel of Christ*. The area in which Timothy has been cooperating with God is 'the gospel of Christ'. This is the only use in 1 Thessalonians of the phase 'the gospel of Christ', and there is much discussion regarding the reasons for its use, and whether this designates Christ as the content or the source of the good news. In 1 Thess. 1.5 the event of 'our' good news (see 2 Thess. 2.14) is associated with divine activity, and all four references in 1 Thess. 2 are to God's good news; they refer 'the gospel of God' to the context of Paul's presentation of apostolic behaviour affirmed and defined by God. The context of the one reference in 2 Thessalonians to 'the gospel of our Lord Jesus' is that of his judgement on those disobedient to the good news. In the letter to the Romans 'gospel of God' and 'gospel of Christ' appear to be used as balancing statements so that the centrality of Christ is matched by the emphasis on God as initiator (Dunn, 1998, p. 166). Probably 'the gospel of Christ' as used in 1 Thess. 3.2 performs the same function; the frequency of 'gospel of God' in 1 Thess. 2 is probably due to the nature of Paul's argument there, where he establishes the missionaries' integrity on the basis of their vocation and authorization by God. Here he can speak of Christ the encourager.

Having stressed at the opening of the narration his own personal agony at being separated from the converts he turns now to the tribulations of the Thessalonians. The purpose in sending Timothy was: *to encourage you to stand firm for the faith and under all these hardships remain unshaken* (3.2c–3a). The REB gives a twofold shape to Timothy's commission. It may well have been twofold, but there is a slightly different division among the phrases. Timothy's first commission is 'to establish' you (the verb can stand alone or with a direct object). 2 Thess. 3.3 recalls the faithful reliability of God who can 'strengthen you and guard you from all evil'. It can be used in the passive, in Rom. 1.11 as the passive of divine action. Rom. 1.11

is an interesting parallel to 1 Thess. 3 since in Rom. 1.11 Paul longs to see those he addresses, to share some spiritual gift with them so God may strengthen them, or for mutual encouragement through each other's faith. This use of the verb, extended from physical support to moral and spiritual support, is well illustrated in the Jewish philosopher Philo's work, where Moses distinguishes Isaac's leadership from Joseph's: the latter 'experiences one counter-attraction after another' and so 'is shaken this way and that and driven so he cannot be stabilized' (Philo, *On Dreams* II.11). The verb 'to strengthen, confirm, stabilize' also plays an important role in two prayer-wish sections (also in a doxology if Rom. 16.25 is included). In 1 Thess. 3.13 the verb has a direct object with an additional complement: 'May he [the Lord Jesus] establish your hearts blameless in holiness in the presence of our God and Father at the coming of our Lord Jesus with all his holy ones.' In another prayer section, 2 Thess. 2.17, inner encouragement for the heart and external strength for action are both represented. The feature of 'stabilizing the community' probably deserves a mention in the translation of Timothy's first commission. He was also, secondly, to exhort them concerning their faith. As we discovered in 1 Thess. 1.3, faith *'pistis'* could mean there the 'corporate faith-event'. Timothy is to do what Paul in 1 Thessalonians is attempting to do, to rehearse the corporate faith-event: that is, to secure the memory of it against various queries and suspicions, and the effectiveness of it against external pressures. What then of the phrase 'to *remain unshaken under all these hardships*' or 'that nobody be agitated in the midst of all these tribulations'? It has sometimes been noted that there is neither a conjunction ('and' or 'but') nor a preposition between that phrase and the two former phrases we have just been considering. Usually translators assume one ('and') or the other (a preposition), or both. But a grammatical explanation of the absence of both conjunction and preposition is as follows: 'that nobody be agitated in the midst of all these tribulations' stands in apposition to what went before, referring back to either the previous phrase or the previous two phrases. 'That nobody be agitated in the midst of all these tribultions' is exegetical of either 'to exhort concerning your faith', or of both 'to stabilize you' and 'exhort concerning your faith'. The latter (that it refers to both phrases) makes very good sense, since we have already met the verb 'stabilize' against the context of Joseph's vacillation, and 'to exhort concerning your corporate faith-event' is necessary because suspicions or queries may cause uncertainty. So

Paul tells the Thessalonians that Timothy's commission (whether as Paul recalls it in retrospect, or as Paul accurately recalled what he told Timothy to do) was: 'to stabilize you and to exhort regarding your corporate faith-event', that is to say, 'that no one be agitated (or shaken) in the midst of these tribulations'. The same construction is to be found at 1 Thess. 4.16, where its interpretation, as here, is important for the understanding of the text.

Once again Paul calls on the memory of the Thessalonians to assist his case. No one should have been unduly agitated or shaken once they recalled what Paul had told them: *You know that this is our appointed lot* (3.3b). That warning he had personally taken to heart (see 'our' appointed lot), and hence was not taken unawares; they should have heeded it too, particularly so since the warning had been frequently given ('when we were with you we were constantly telling you beforehand'), and given in terms that pointed to the unavoidability of hardships for those who follow Christ ('we were bound to suffer'; Wanamaker, p. 131). Paul adds a comment from more recent times: just *as it has* in fact *turned out* [the 'happening' verb again] and as you yourselves know (3.4). Paul is using the narration as a means of communicating his own feelings and thoughts, as much as recording what happened in sequence. So the thought of the inevitability of suffering takes him back again to the moment when he despatched Timothy. *This is why I could bear it no longer* [see 3.1] *and sent to find out about your faith* (3.5a). What is on Paul's mind is what he had described in 2.17–20 (see also Phil. 2.16): his anxiety that through the Satan's work what promised future, glorious joy might turn out to be a fruitless and ineffective disaster: *I was afraid that the tempter* had perhaps already *tempted you and our labour* become [the 'happening' verb] *wasted* (3.5).

Paul might be thought to be more taken up with his own feelings and concerns than with the difficulties which the Thessalonians might be having. The argument which we have followed through the opening chapters puts a different slant on that apparent personal preoccupation. The Thessalonian event, in which he and his colleagues had played a part, was decisive for the Thessalonians and for the Gentile mission too. Hence Paul's concern that Jewish opponents as well as townsfolk had tried to obstruct him. For the Thessalonian event to prove a failure was unthinkable, since it was a divinely appointed moment of election for the Gentiles. If he was concerned that his own labour might have become fruitless, and if he was caught up in his own personal agonies, he was so because in that period of his separation from the Thessalonians the future of God's own work was at stake. That could not fail. And as Paul will say a little later, for him (Paul) what happened and what was happening in Thessalonica was a life and death matter. In that respect, too, his was a pattern to follow.

The narration continues in 3.6–10 without any indication of the movements of Paul, Silvanus and Timothy, or any mention of how Paul copes with the intervening period. It resumes the story with all three in Corinth, Timothy having recently returned from Thessalonica, and Paul dictating 1 Thessalonians by way of response to Timothy's good news: *But now Timothy has just returned from his visit to you, bringing good news of your faith and love* (3.6). The opening word 'But' reminds us of the contrast between Paul's agonizing over the thought of 'wasted labour' and the new situation with Timothy's return. Everything has changed with what Paul describes as Timothy's 'good news'. The description 'good news' brings Timothy's report into the orbit of the gospel message, and with good reason. What has not changed is the evidence of the astonishing event in Thessalonica; the Thessalonians' 'faith and love' which Paul held in thankful remembrance in 1.3 remain as a central feature of Timothy's report. Their 'faith and love' *is* the gospel message (see the commentary on 1.5), along with the good remembrance of Paul and his colleagues which the Thessalonians maintain permanently (the REB translation *he tells us you always think kindly of us* (3.6) is a little too weak). 'Remembrance' completes a fresh triad along with faith and love; it includes a recollection of the Thessalonians' pattern of living, which initially gave such a ringing endorsement of God's word (1.6–8); and it involves the mutuality, unaffected by the time of separation, of the longing (see the REB at Phil. 1.8 and Rom. 1.11), each for the other, which all involved in the happenings in Thessalonica continue to share: *'longing to see us as we are to see you'* (3.6c).

Often the absence in 3.6 of 'hope', the third member of the triad in 1.3, is taken to be a change in the Thessalonians' condition: in respect of 'faith and love' they remain committed to their initial vision, but Timothy cannot say the same of their 'hope'. If, however 'remembrance' carries the weight we have suggested, 'hope' remains part of their vision, and had Timothy made that report it is difficult to see how Paul could have expected the Thessalonians with that loss of vision to have shared with him the prayer of 3.17. 2 Thess. 1.3 also lacks 'hope' as a third member of a triad (the reference to 'faith and love' is extended into 1.4); but in 1.5 the theme is taken up of 'worthiness for the kingdom of God'. Triads are common in the Thessalonian correspondence, and Paul seems to have employed considerable creativity in their development (see Introduction, section 11). It is therefore more than likely that the triad in 1 Thess. 3.6 is 'faith', 'love', 'remembrance', with 'remembrance' having taken a prior place in Timothy's report – or perhaps 'remembrance', in Paul's hearing of Timothy's report, claimed major attention for what above everything concerned Paul. There is no doubt that the Thessalonians' understanding of the future needed to benefit from Paul's powerful grasp of the issues. But that is a very different matter from the claim that the Thessalonians had lost their vision of a future hope.

Once again we encounter the problem of how long, extended and involved sentences can happily be translated for public reading. In the original Greek 1 Thess. 3.6–8 is a single sentence, whereas in the REB it forms four separate sentences. What can we learn from the original Greek about the relationship of the four sentences? We noted that the opening word 'but' in 3.6 probably marks the contrast between Paul's agonizing over the thought of 'wasted labour' in 3.1–5 and the new situation brought by Timothy's return. Further, we have seen that the new situation was caused by Timothy's good news, summarized in the triad 'faith, love, remembrance'. The consequence of all this is given in 3.7: *So amid all our difficulties and hardships* [as in 2 Cor. 6.4, a fresh word in 1 Thessalonians] *we are reassured* [comforted or consoled in respect to you: see the use of the word in 2 Cor. 1.4–6], *my friends, by the news of your faith* [presumably 'faith' in its widest possible corporate sense]. Notable in this consequence of Timothy's report is that Paul reverts to the difficulties and hardships he had experienced (in other words, to the focus of 3.1–5); he has been consoled, with all the implications of this for the Christian mission among Gentiles. Finally, Paul strengthens his comment that he is 'reassured' by adding: *It is the breath of life to us to know that you stand fast in the Lord* (3.8). The general sense of this conclusion is clear: news that the Thessalonians stand firm reinvigorates Paul and his colleagues. That is a fairly commonplace comment in the 'friendly' style of ancient letters. Even if we render the sentence literally, that remains the case: 'we live, if you stand in the Lord'. It sounds somewhat of an epistolary cliché. But is that how Paul intended the conclusion to be heard? For him 'life' can be a much more intense expression. In 2 Cor. 1.8–9 he comments on the trouble he had experienced in the province of Asia:

> The burden of it was far too heavy for us to bear, so heavy that we even despaired of life. Indeed, we felt in our hearts that we had received a death sentence. This was meant to teach us to place reliance not on ourselves, but on God who raises the dead. From such mortal peril God delivered us; and he will deliver us again.

Just as 'remembrance' in 3.6 carries a vast array of theological implications, so 'life' does here. The epistolary cliché is capable of a transformed meaning. Some scholars who have gathered together the range of epistolary expressions in the Thessalonian correspondence have used this valuable research as a means of monitoring the letters' level of expression, sometimes hesitating to move far beyond the level of the epistolary. A translation such as 'the breath of life', evocative though it is, only takes us a short distance from the epistolary level. A quite different stratum of thought and expression emerges in the parallel passage just quoted from 2 Cor. 1. In all probability 'life' means in 1 Thess. 3.8, as it does in 2 Cor. 1, that God has breathed new life into the missionaries, virtually a resurrection experience, as the work which seemed endangered (3.5) had become, evidently, alive with the vibrancy they all remembered from their arrival in Thessalonica (3.6): 'For we now live, if indeed you stand firm in the Lord.'

It is true that such 'remembrance' is a feature of the kind of letter a mentor in the ancient world might write, encompassing memory, feelings, imitation, self-commitment and teaching (Malherbe, pp. 209–10). On the other hand, even that rich area of reference may not do justice to the particular circumstances in which Paul is writing. What follows adds into the picture the particularities of Paul's faith, which give the epistolary language, particularly evident in this section of the letter, a distinctive content and emphasis.

The third thanksgiving
3.9–10

Another long sentence follows in the Greek text, a rhetorical question composed of vv. 9–10 and beginning *What thanksgiving can we give to God in return . . . ?* The first thanksgiving to God was part of

43

a continuous mutual recollection in 1 Thess. 1.2–10 of the remarkable events in Thessalonica. The second thanksgiving flowed from
the mutual recollection of the response of the Thessalonians to all
the work of the missionaries (2.10–12), a response recognizing that
God was at work there (2.13), and so genuine that it involved following the example of the Judaean churches. In 1 Thess. 3.9–10,
the third of the thanksgiving references, Paul asks what thanksgiving to God would be sufficient to respond to the divine generosity in what has now happened. What has happened (according
to 1 Thess. 2.17—3.8) is the confirmation of those initial events in
Thessalonica; and despite all the hindrances and hardships which
all have experienced, both converts and missionaries, the divinely
appointed work of God still carries its promise of fruitfulness, glory
and joy. What thanksgiving could possibly match such events? The
answer must be: none! (O'Brien, p. 156). But the picture of that
thanksgiving is not yet complete.

The thanksgiving to God is particularly for the Thessalonians.
Their faith, love and remembrance is a cause for great joy: *What
thanks for all the joy you have brought us, making us rejoice before our
God . . . ?* (3.9b). 'Joy' in the writings of Paul brings together, as
we have seen, many different factors. Here it wells up 'before our
God' as a consequence of what God has done (Rom. 15.13). This
has its parallels in the worship patterns of the Old Testament and
intertestamental period (see Isa. 66.10; Ps. 126; Tobit 11.15–17).
Joy has strong associations with the work of the Holy Spirit (1
Thess. 1.3; Rom. 14.17), and with peace, wholeness and faith (Phil.
1.25). It is both an individual and a shared experience (2 Cor. 2.3;
7.13). Joy can be shared, since, rather than remaining as an inner
emotion, it is expressed externally by all manner of means; here in
1 Thessalonians it is expressed as form and content within the letter. It coexists with perseverance and patience (Col. 1.11). Lastly, it
is an anticipation of the final joy, which celebrates the fulfilment of
the divine purpose, in its association with the marriage feast and
feasting. In 1 Thessalonians it belongs in the presence of God here
and now (3.11) and in God's presence at the fulfilment of his purposes: 2.19–20. Joy is therefore one of the signs of and awareness
of divine reliability and faithfulness in a world where uncertainty
seems to reign (see Charles Wesley's hymn, 'Love Divine, all loves
excelling', and its second line, referring to the incarnation of the
source of all love: 'Joy of heaven to earth come down').

1 Thess. 3.10 draws in yet another association, that of prayer (see

Phil. 1.4). The Thessalonians' remembrance of Paul quickens both his delight and also his desire to visit them; so Paul and Silvanus rejoice before God and doubt they can adequately thank God, as *'we pray* with the utmost earnestness *night and day to be allowed to see you again'* (3.10a). That leads almost immediately to the prayer-wish of 3.11–13 which asks precisely for that (3.11). Paul's concern to visit them again has coloured the previous 14 verses; but it cannot be accidental that the utmost earnestness of Paul's prayers, day and night, spills out into the text of the letter, and does so as a prayer that the way to Thessalonica may be divinely opened. But between 3.10a and 3.11 there is a further motivation for the visit: *and to make good whatever is lacking in your faith* (3.10b). What Paul has in mind has been much discussed and various solutions offered. There is little specific indication in 1 Thessalonians of what was seriously lacking, and much that Paul writes about the Thessalonians suggests they have a full and rounded faith. So when Timothy was sent to them it was to confirm them in their faith. Moreover 'to make good' may well sell both writer and hearer short. The aim of both is not what is satisfactory, but what meets ultimate standards: 'to bring to completion your faith's shortcomings'. It is at least possible that just as 3.10a is picked up with the prayer in 3.11, the pastoral concern expressed in 3.10b is picked up by Paul in the second and third parts of the prayer of 3.12–13. That is to say: 'what is lacking' are the further steps in the range and intensity of their love, and a deeper understanding of what is means to 'stand before God . . . when our Lord Jesus comes' (O'Brien, p. 159).

The first prayer-wish
3.11–13

The five prayers in the Thessalonian letters begin in a similar way: *May our God and Father himself* (3.11), 'May God himself' (5.23), and see 2 Thess. 2.15–17; 3.5; 3.16. One of the close Pauline parallels to these prayer-wishes is Rom. 15.13: 'And may God, who is the ground of hope, fill you with all joy and peace as you lead the life of faith, until, by the power of the Holy Spirit, you overflow with hope' (see also Rom. 15.33). All these examples are not prayer units formed independently of the text. They are built into and from the context by the author as he moves into the language of prayer. 1 Thess. 3.11 does so not only by praying *open the way for us to come*

45

to you, but by recognizing that such a prayer has three important dimensions which the letter has already explored. First, the context of all life and work is God the Father and the Lord Jesus Christ (1.1a) to whom also we owe grace and peace (1.1b). Second, the letter stresses the importance of the relationship of the missionaries and the Thessalonians; it recalls the context of thanksgiving to God in which the mutual relationships, established in the events in Thessalonica, are celebrated, the fulfilment of which will be in the presence of God: 'when we stand before our Lord Jesus at his coming' (2.16). Third, the prayer for 'an opening of the way' is against the background of threats to the progress of the gospel of God and of Christ (2.2; 3.2). The prayer is appropriate because of all those facets of the letter as a whole, as well as because of the immediate context. There the desire for face-to-face meeting has quickened, the hindrances have been divinely overcome and the response has become a joyful, if inadequate thanksgiving (3.9). God's directing of his servant's path is a theme of the Psalms (see Ps. 5.8), and Paul prays that this may lead to Thessalonica: 'may he direct our paths to you'.

As for you (presumably whether or not Paul can visit them), *may the Lord make your love increase and overflow to one another and to everyone, as our love does to you* (3.12). Again Paul and his colleagues are the model, and the Thessalonians are to follow their example. The one who can help them follow that example and make their love overflow is, however, 'the Lord' (presumably in the light of the previous verse and the following verse, the Lord Jesus). In 1 Thess. 4.9–12 the 'overflowing of love' among the Thessalonians is acknowledged, but the prayer asks that love's extension and broadening should be taken still further. What Paul means precisely by that we must consider later, although it is clear that this love should overflow 'to one another and to everyone'. The prayer-wish opens up a theme which is to be developed later. There is a passage in the letter to the Philippians which resembles this prayer-wish closely; the vocabulary there may differ in some cases from 1 Thess. 3.12–13, but the similarity of the contents is striking:

God knows how I long for you all with the deep yearning of Christ Jesus himself. And this is my prayer, that your love may grow ever richer in knowledge and insight of every kind enabling you to learn by experience what things really matter. Then on the day of Christ you will be flawless and without blame. (Phil. 1.8–10)

It would seem likely that this is close to what Paul intended when he wrote of 'what is lacking' or 'where your faith stops short'.

The third part of the prayer-wish (3.13), like Phil. 1.10, links the overflowing of love with the ultimate purpose of Christian living: May he make your love increase so as to *make your hearts firm, so that you can stand before our God and Father holy and faultless when our Lord comes with all* his holy ones (3.13). The overflowing of love has an immediate and present significance. It has also in the longer view a part to play in our preparation for the future. We have considered earlier how demanding it must have seemed for Gentiles (especially if they had not passed through the intermediate stage of being God-fearers) to be expected 'to stand holy and faultless before our God and Father'. Holiness belongs to God as the Psalms emphasize: 'Give thanks to his holy name' (Ps. 30.4); 'Rejoice in the Lord and bless his holy name (Ps. 97.12); and in the Septuagint of the Psalms: 'Thanksgiving and beauty are before him; holiness and majesty in his holy place' (95.6); 'They will tell of the majesty of your glorious holiness and will recount your wonderful deeds (144.5). To stand before God, our whole selves 'blameless in holiness', creates an unbelievable picture, yet this picture is an important link between this prayer-wish here at the end of the first section of the letter, and the second prayer-wish in 1 Thess. 5.23. There however, in 5.23, part of Paul's answer is given to all the Christians in Thessalonica who might doubt the possibility of such an outcome of Christian living: 'May God himself, the God of peace, make you holy through and through.'

The complexities of Paul's response to the Thessalonians are slowly beginning to emerge. The Thessalonians have been chosen and called (1.4), destined for the full attainment of salvation through the Lord Jesus Christ (5.10). Abandonment to human fate and its limited, fallible resources is not for them (1.10). The resources of Jesus Christ are in their daily participation in Christ's dying and perseverance, in the restoration of true humanity through that sharing in Christ, and in the ultimate security of the one whom God raised from the dead. God has called them through Christ, and to a holiness of life through the work of the Holy Spirit (4.7). Part of that growth in holiness is through the strengthening of faith and love (3.12). For love makes possible the strengthening of Christian living, enlivening emotion, will, perceptiveness, action, sharing and community (4.9–12). The apostolic model presents the possibility of devout, just and blameless living (2.10) which summons those who are called to follow in that way. But the fruitfulness and effectiveness of this pattern of living is only truly known when standing before the Lord Christ in the glory and joy of his coming (2.19). A share in the kingdom of God is for those who are worthy of the kingdom and reliant on God's gift of holiness (2.12; 5.23); it is, together with Christ and all the holy ones (1 Thess. 4.10—5.6), a life shaped by his presence and holiness (5.23; Barton pp. 193–213).

The questions which arise for us from such an answer are different from those of the Thessalonians. The events in Thessalonica were experienced as a divine act of deliverance from humanity's structure of self-imprisonment. What is ultimate was reached by them within a limited framework of space and time. Paul himself has to wrestle with the issue of God's faithfulness to Israel, and probably stayed, at the stage of the Thessalonian correspondence, with the belief that the opposition to the Gentile mission was not an ultimate disaster for Israel. The kingdom is God's victorious gathering of a holy people through the work of Christ, Lord and Son. Our concern is, as was Paul's, for the salvation of all humanity, and we glimpse a possibility in Paul's Thessalonian work of the hope of humanity's restoration in Christ and in the patterns of grace by which an ultimate hope for humanity can be sustained. Our difficulty is with our structures of space and time, and with the complexity of human relationships, which we glimpsed in the Introduction.

We sense in Paul's picture of a vibrant Christian community a pattern of relevance today, especially in the picture which is emerging of a community with commitment and responsibilities in love to the surrounding and ever-widening area. But we should want to look more closely at the meaning and practical expressions of love, so love does not become self-congratulatory and destructive of the potential of others for their vocation and style of being. This will be a feature of Part Two.

1 Thessalonians
PART TWO

Called to holiness
4.1-8

The shape of the second part of 1 Thessalonians is like the river in
Smetana's tone poem *Ma Vlast*. It flows from its source, weaving
through different terrains and landscapes, finally to empty itself
in full flood into the sea. 1 Thess. 4–5 is like that: it flows from its
source in 3.12–13 through several areas of interest and concern,
identifiable in what has been called 'Paul's lexicon of exhortation'
(Malherbe, p. 218), and finally commits itself to the sanctifying
work of the faithful God.

The opening words of 4.1 give us no indication of where we are;
they could be translated: 'Further then', or 'Finally now', or, 'Well
then', or as in the REB, *And now, friends, we have* some things *to ask
of you*. Paul adds that he will also exhort them (see 4.10; 5.14) on
the basis of traditions he has given them: *We passed on to you the
tradition* (4.1b), a tradition concerning appropriate behaviour: *the
way we must live* (4.1c). The phrase 'the way you must live' and the
following phrase *if we are to please God* (4.1d) use the terms which
we met earlier in the letter in Paul's confirmation that he seeks only
to please God who is continually testing our hearts (2.4), and in his
exhortation that the Thessalonians should live worthily of 'the God
who called you into his kingdom and glory' (2.12). The character
of the tradition which Paul himself uses in 1 Thess. 2, and the language which, according to 4.1, characterized the tradition he taught
them previously in Thessalonica, 'on how to live' and 'on pleasing
God', has a distinctively Jewish ring (see Gen. 6.9: 'Noah was a
righteous man, the one blameless man of his time, and he walked
with God', and, in the Septuagint 'he pleased God'; Ecclus 44.16:
'Enoch pleased the Lord and was taken up to heaven'; Ps. 116.9:
'I will walk in the presence of the Lord in the land of the living',

rephrased in the Septuagint 'I will be well pleasing in the presence of God in the land of the living'; also Ps. 55.14). Paul understands the Christian community as accepting and adapting patterns of corporate behaviour with deep Jewish roots. That is true also of several other verses in this chapter, as we shall note in due course.

This emphasis on the adaptation of Jewish roots in Paul's traditions regarding social behaviour needs to be placed in a wider context. First, there is the question of the hearers of the letter in Thessalonica and their background. So far in 1 Thessalonians Paul has given particular attention to the Gentile or non-Jewish converts. Much of 1 Thess. 4.1–12 would have a particular appeal to Jewish Christians, and might answer some of the reservations about Paul's teaching, which Jewish Christians most probably had. The letter is intended for the entire Christian community in Thessalonica (5.27), and we may be witnessing in 1 Thess. 4.1–12 Paul's concern that his letter should contribute to their peace and harmony. Second, extant in Paul's time were Graeco-Roman traditions, sometimes dealing with similar areas of social concern to the Jewish traditions. We need to formulate how far Paul knew and took account of these parallel traditions, and, just as important, how well they were known among the Thessalonians. There is some evidence to suggest that in a city such as Thessalonica only the elite were conversant with Graeco-Roman discussions of social topics, and we have seen many of the Gentile converts would not have enjoyed those kind of privileges, either economic or intellectual. Third, Paul's social instructions function within the deracination which we have earlier described. In such a disturbed area of social life they could have functioned divisively in challenging pagan morality (see 4.4); but, alternatively, they could have assisted the converts to find new patterns of belonging and identity. Fourth, there is evidence of overlaps of social teaching between various parts of the New Testament; this has led some scholars to posit catechetical material some of which has early Christian moral teaching. Whether the Thessalonian correspondence was influenced by such bodies of material is not clear. There are no catalogues or moral codes in these letters. Fifth, there is the question of how Paul structured his moral teaching. Certainly he believed in the power of example, as the emphasis on 'imitation' shows in 1 Thessalonians and in the standards of bahaviour set out in 1 Thess. 2.1–16. He also worked with moral principles, such as the triads he developed; he illustrated how these might be related to different specific situations (see Rom. 12.9–10). In discussion of social behaviour he used precepts, as many of the Graeco-Roman philosophers did. Seneca wrote to Lucilius:

> Precepts are the food on which the inward powers thrive and grow; they supplement intuitive knowledge with fresh convictions and set right false conceptions . . . once afforded championship and the aid precepts can give, the natural talent surmounts its difficulties, provided always that the mischief is not of so long-standing as to have utterly poisoned or destroyed it. (Letter 94)

These examples illustrate the need for powers of discrimination, of the kind at which Paul hints in 5.21. Sixth, there are the questions of perception of the right ways to live and how transformation makes such changes of life-style possible. Apart from 'imitation' there is also in the Thessalonian letters awareness of 'participation' as a key factor in transformation. 'He became what we are that we may become what he truly is' has been used as an interpretative tool for 1 Thess. 5.10 (Hooker-Stacey, p. 165), and the areas of perseverance and faithfulness illustrate such transformative patterns. As part of that interpretative pattern in 1 Thess. 5.10 there is the activity of God whose love seeks the salvation of those he calls. This gives an ultimacy to love, as also the work of God's Holy Spirit gives ultimacy to holiness, understood in relation to loving action, the dynamic power to change human life (see 4.7–8).

A seventh consideration leads us into the final phrases of 1 Thess. 4.1. These transformative features of Paul's moral teaching illuminate the emphasis which we have already noted in 3.12, and which appears twice in 4.1–12: *you are indeed following it* [i.e. the way to live], *but we beg you to do so yet more thoroughly* (4.1ef). The same Greek term *'perisseuo'* ('abound') which we find in 3.12 and 4.1, is also used in 4.10: 'You are in fact practising the rule of love towards all your fellow Christians . . . Yet we appeal to you friends, to do better still.' 'More thoroughly'; and 'better still' capture part of Paul's vision. As we noted in 3.10–12 this is a call for 'abundant living'. Paul's moral traditions look for and ask for an overflowing of love as well as the desire to please God. There is an immeasurable character to the call for holiness, as there is to the divine activity that calls the new life into being. So both the references to moral traditions in 4.1–2 are characterized by references to Jesus Christ. They are passed on 'in the Lord Jesus' and '*You know the* precepts *we gave you* through *the Lord Jesus'* (4.2). Both phrases mark out the context in which the traditions are given, and those contexts have been touched on in several of the seven considerations listed above. How far Paul envisaged the Lord as the origin of any of these traditions is not clear. Some consonance between the Jesus traditions in the Gospels regarding behaviour and Paul's moral teaching can hardly be denied. But such factual and historical considerations take second place behind the summons to and the means of transformation.

The principle concerning holiness and a practical precept follows: *This is the will of God, that you should* practise holiness: *you must abstain from fornication* (4.3). As we saw in 3.10–12 'holiness' is a numinous, dynamic separateness, calling for separateness for those who are the elect, who are being set aside for God's service, and entailing dispositional responses or transformed possibilities as both context and potential. The particular response which the precept calls to mind is one element in the Apostolic Council's letter in Acts 15.23–29 (Barrett, pp. 732–46): 'Abstain . . . from porneia (fornication, or immorality)'. Its appearance in the *Testament of the Twelve Patriarchs* (TestReuben 5.5) and in *1 Clement* 30.1 reminds us of the broad area of moral teaching to which this precept belongs. The term *'porneia'* commonly means prostitution, fornication, uncleanness, although in 1 Cor. 5.1 it has reference to a particular sexual irregularity (see 1 Cor. 6.18, where 'sexual immorality' is an appropriate translation). In 1 Thess. 4.3 the more general term 'immorality' is preferable, and the Greek use of the definite article with it may support that view.

There are three possible interpretations of 4.4. The first is, as in the REB, to take the Greek word *'skeuos'* to mean 'body': *each one of you must learn to gain mastery of his body, to hallow and honour it.* This, however, strains the meaning of the verb, which means 'acquiring' rather than 'mastering' (the verb only means 'master' in the sense of 'one who has acquired'), and it omits the very strong reflexive pronoun 'his own body'. Those two difficulties question also the much more specific translation of *'skeuos'* which is sometimes suggested – 'the male sexual member'. Perhaps the best translation is: 'to possess one's own wife in sanctification and honour', since Ecclus 36.24 (in the Hebrew, 36.25) provides excellent support for translating the verb 'possess' (see also 1 Cor. 7.2), and the translaton fits the reflexive pronoun very appropriately (again, see 1 Cor. 7.2). The translation 'possess' emphasizes the durative sense of the verb; that is, the verse is about the continuity of marriage rather than entry into marriage. The word *'skeuos'* ('thing', 'vessel') is a disrespectful reference to a 'wife' in today's world, but 1 Pet. 3.7 writes of 'the weaker womanly *skeuos'*, and Prov. 5.15–18 and rabbinic literature provide ample analogies. If the expression seems strange to us (and we wonder if Paul's hearers would have picked up the reference to marriage) it draws renewed attention to Paul's claim to have already in the past given them this traditional teaching. What then does 'to possess one's wife in sanctification and honour' mean? 1 Thess. 4.5 gives a negative impression of 'sanctification and honour' – *not giving way to lust like the pagans who know nothing of God* (4.5). As in 1 Cor. 7 Paul is depicting marriage as a means of controlling, even eliminating, lust, and thereby setting a boundary between the converts and the rest of humankind. In fact Paul's concern was shared at least partially within his intellectual environment. Sensuality was of course a feature of many forms of Roman religion, but a philosopher like Seneca could regard the sexual urge as a form of disorder, and other philosophers could point to the political weaknesses in a person who yielded to his bodily cravings. Scholars who have given particular attention to Jewish writers such as Philo, who sought to express his Jewish values and beliefs within a Hellenistic context, see a genuine correlation between Paul's sharp distaste for Gentile sexual conduct and 'Jewish selective Hellenism' (Tomson, p. 111). While the negative interpretation which Paul adds in 4.5 is important, the positive recommendation 'in sanctification and honour' should not be reduced to that alone. Sanctification carries the implications of concern, care and affection for others, and of honour (in Paul's critique of his competitive world) and respect for the fate of others, a view which is found in the Graeco-Roman tradition also. There are further implications, too, both positive and negative, but those lead us into the next verse, 1 Thess. 4.6: *'No one must do his fellow-Christian wrong in this matter, or infringe his rights.'* In the Greek this verse is parallel in its construction to what we found in 3.3. There we suggested that it clarified the previous statement or statements. If that is the case here, then 4.6 clarifies 4.5 and so both concern matters of sex and marriage. The two verbs translated in the REB 'do wrong' and 'infringe rights' mean basically 'transgress' and 'overreach, take advantage of' (see 2 Cor. 2.11; 12.17) respectively. With 'brother' (here a Christian brother) as object of each verb, and retaining the context of sexual morality, the two verbs can refer to stealing a Christian brother's wife. The second of the verbs *'pleonektein'* ('rob') is used in philosophical dis-cussion of adultery, for example of the taking of Menelaus' Helen to Troy. That particular meaning fits well with the reference in 4.6b to God's punishing of all such offences (see the Holiness Code, and especially Leviticus 17—25). The whole section, 4.3–8, can be seen as a unit with a single main topic, holiness and sexuality (see espe-cially 4.7). Of course, a case can be made for regarding 'this matter' in 4.6a as commercial, and then *'pleonektein'* has the well-attested sense of 'defrauding'. But the arguments above for the single topic in 4.3–8 of holiness and sexuality probably compose the stronger case. 1 Thess. 4.7: *For God called us to holiness, not to impurity* could fit with either a sexual context or a commercial one, since both are features of the Levitical Holiness Code. 'Akatharsia' has already been used in the sense of 'impurity' by Paul himself, as we have argued regarding 2.3.

The conclusion of the unit in 4.8 makes the link between what is taught and how what is taught can be realized, that is, between the precepts which Paul had given, and the gift of the Holy Spirit: *Anyone therefore who flouts these* precepts *is flouting not man but God who bestows on you his Holy Spirit*. Here the authority of Paul's tra-ditional teaching is divine. Because they are traditions handed on from person to person they are not thereby of human origin and weight. They carry God's authority (see 4.8). The REB carefully uses the present tense of God bestowing the Holy Spirit. This is not a reference backward in time to the 'Thessalonica event' and to the initial gift of the Spirit, but a reminder of the continuous work of the Holy Spirit in the lives of the converts. Using a phrase reminis-cent of Ezek. 37.6 and 14, Paul writes of God putting the Holy Spirit collectively into their lives. It is a transforming work, and perhaps incremental (that is, it is an addition to the divine authorization of the moral teaching): some Greek texts read (and it is perhaps the better reading) '[God], who also puts his Holy Spirit into you'. What God requires he also enables the converts to achieve through the inner working of the Holy Spirit.

Love of the 'friends'
4.9–12

About love of the brotherhood (4.9) could be Paul's reply to a written document brought by Timothy from Thessalonica ('About' in 1 Corinthians introduces a reply to written issues in a sequence of sections; see 1 Cor. 7.1). Alternatively Paul may have chosen this general heading to deal with specific points which Timothy had raised. Paul had already raised the subject of 'love of one another' in the prayer-wish in 3.12, where it has the form 'love for one another and to everyone'.

'Love of the "friends"' in 4.1 is a translation of the single word *'philadelphia'*, and what follows in 4.9–10 seems to concentrate attention at least initially on internal relationships within the Christian community or between Christian communities. *'Philadelphia'* understood as inner-community charity, 'love of the "friends"' in that sense, is an appropriate heading for the unit. The term *'philadelphia'* is found in the same sense also in Rom. 12.10 (see Heb. 13.1 which extends beyond *'philadelphia'* into hospitality, visiting those in prison and caring for the ill-treated). So in Paul it seems to imply initially inner-Christian charity. Elsewhere in the ancient world the meaning of *philadelphia* was different. In Hellenistic philosophical writings it refers to sibling love; Plutarch's essay 'Concerning *Philadelphia*' is offered to two brothers as a special gift; Josephus uses *'philadelphia'* of Joseph's brothers (and sometimes negatively of 'nepotism'); Philo and the Septuagint use it similarly of sibling love. These prefer the similar term *'philanthropia'* when they wish to refer to the common moral context of love towards human beings, or in Josephus' case in reference to the Mosaic law (that is, of animals as well as humans). For distinctively Jewish group behaviour (such as among the Essenes and Pharisees) Josephus uses the term 'lovers of one another'. The early Christian use of *'philadelphia'* for inner-Christian charity is therefore noteworthy. That is not to say that early Christianity was unconcerned with hospitality, with the needy, those in prison and the poor. On the contrary, early Christian literature gives outstanding examples of all these. It is simply that *'philadelphia'* as a moral term concentrates initially on inner-community love. As we shall see, 4.11–12 recognizes the implications of such inner-Christian love and how this is expressed in practical terms. In 4.11–12 questions are raised which are paralleled in the early Christian document, the Didache.

The Didache regulates for apostolic visits (see 1 Thess. 2.9), for other Christian visitors and for those who wish to settle so as not to cause too great a burden on the local Christian community. For anyone who 'wishes to settle' the regulation is: 'if he has a trade, let him work and eat' (Didache 12.3; see 2 Thess. 3.10). Behind that regulation we can presuppose a common table at which all who work can eat, and the needy should not be turned away (Didache 4.8). We shall find a similar pattern in rabbinic models. So when in 1 Thess. 4.9 Paul turns to *'philadelphia'* he turns to a pattern of Judaeo-Christian moral teaching which includes institutional features, and to which those in different strata of Thessalonian economic, social and intellectual life may relate (Tomson [Hooker-Stacey] pp. 122–4).

Concerning 'love of the "friends"' *you need no words of mine, for you are yourselves taught by God to love one another . . .* (4.9b). Typical of letters contemporary with Paul's is to say no instruction is required on a particular matter but then to proceed to give it. That is what happens here. They do not need instruction for a remarkable reason, given by a single word in Greek: they are 'taught by God', a word which Paul may well have invented. It underlines the divine authority behind Judaeo-Christian moral teaching, as indicated in 4.8. It also underlines the centrality of mutual love, by tracing it back to its divine origin (2 Thess. 3.5). In one respect the Thessalonians have taken this particular area of teaching to heart: *you are in fact practising this rule of love towards all your* brothers *throughout Macedonia* (4.10). The details of such practice of loving concern are unknown to us; except that we have seen the early stages of this work in 1 Thess. 1.2–8 and in the participation of Macedonian churches in the Collection for the Saints; there was support from Philippi for Paul in Thessalonica (Phil. 4.16) and from Macedonia for Paul in Corinth (2 Cor. 11.7–11, although that was after the Thessalonian correspondence). We noted the period of time during which Timothy and Silvanus remained in Macedonia, and Timothy's visit to them (see also Rom. 16.1–2). It would be impossible to envisage such cooperation, travel and missionary work across Macedonia without the availability of considerable hospitality (Burke, p. 223), and some would add, patronage. The evidence of charity across Macedonia falls into the pattern of the Judaeo-Christian tradition and we assume sufficient hospitable activity to recognize the validity of Paul's claim.

How 1 Thess. 4.9–10a relate precisely to 4.10b–12 is a matter of dispute. Some scholars consider 4.10b as the beginning of a new subject. But we have already seen how the subject of 'love of the "friends"' finds practical expression in matters relating to manual labour. The REB translation at 4.10b is useful, too, in that it gives the impression in 4.10b not of a fresh beginning but of a corrective to the previous general claim: *Yet we appeal to you, friends, to do better still*. As a correction it performs the same function as do the last three words of 4.1 (see also 3.12); and, as we saw in 4.1, the correction opens the door to an exhilarating prospect. 'To do better still' has the caution of a school report. What Paul is asking for is a releasing of the energies of love to a greater degree than had seemed possible hitherto, and recognition of the detailed care which would be necessary to achieve that. The strong continuity of thought throughout 4.9–12 is illustrated by the Greek of 4.11–12. There, five infinitives each in turn carry the thought of the section further (Ellingworth, p. 88). First, love will abound as *your ambition* rises. Paul constantly uses contemporary language in a re-coded form. That is the case here. 'Ambition' might carry with it for some people the hope of building a reputation, gaining honour and winning a high regard from those in positions of power, and, positively, making a contribution to the life of the city and country; for others, ambition of that kind could result in a disturbed existence, and it would be far better to live a contemplative life: 'The very first precept was: to seek stillness. For that is the light of philosophy, whereas politics and meddlesomeness wrap it in gloom and make the way to philosophy hard for those who search' (Chion's 1C CE epistolary novel, 16.5). Paul's re-coding of 'ambition' is to be heard against both backgrounds. Second, to make possible the abounding of community love one must be ambitious to live a quiet life, to keep a low profile (Wanamaker, p. 163). Aware of all the problems attached to that style of life, Seneca wrote of retirement in the Letter to Lucilius 55: 'loss of direction, self-contentment, living for oneself', problems which a corporate and mutual concern for each other and deep friendships would meet. Third, a low profile would allow time and attention to be given to one's 'own affairs'. (As for time, see Seneca Letter 78. 'For the instructed a single day is more spacious than is the longest day for the layman.' As for attention, that secures the best result for the task in hand.)

So far, a Roman letter-writer has provided possible links of which Paul would have been aware when talking in this way of inner-community care. But it is the fourth link which benefits most from the sequence, and which contributes most to the abundance of community love: It is *'in work with your hands, as we told you'* (4.11c). This provides at least some income, however small it may be, taking the weight from others and contributing to the hospitality and care for those poorer still. From such small actions comes the abundance God seeks. Moreover, the policy of a low profile is seen to its advantage; it is a profile which gains respect for the work done and the sense of responsibility shown: *so that you may gain the respect of those outside your number, and at the same time never be in want* (4.12). Paul has illustrated the relationship between that style of living and love for 'the friends': 'night and day we worked for a living, rather than be a burden to any of you while we proclaimed to you the good news of God' (2.9). The instruction to 'work with the hands' and so make provision for hospitality and the care of the needy is rooted in and belongs within the Judaeo-Christian tradition. Although some of the connecting links within the section can be assumed from Paul's Graeco-Roman environment, the fundamental argument of the passage is shared by Paul with early Christianity and lived out in his own example.

It is often assumed that Christian behaviour has to be dynamic in the sense of spectacular, and that change has to be sudden and dramatic. Paul was impressed by the dynamic opening stages of the work in Thessalonica; but what he asks for now has something of the obedient, careful selflessness which Simone Weil and Iris Murdoch saw as an important challenge to the chaos around.

Together with Christ
4.13 — 5.11

1 Thess. 4.1–12 has presented Paul's counsel regarding two closely related topics, holiness and love of 'the friends'. 4.13—5.11 recommends mutual counsel, each of the sections 4.13–18 and 5.1–11 ending in the same way: 'Counsel (or, console) one another' (4.18 and 5.11). Such mutual counsel relates in both those sections to 'being with the Lord' (4.17d; 5.10c). Both sections make mention of death; the first is specifically about those who had died (4.13–14), and the second is specifically inclusive of the living and the dead. Both sections mention the death of Jesus, and the first belief in Jesus' death and resurrection (4.14). The parallelism between 4.13–18 and 5.1–11 is clearly intentional.

Death in 4.13 is a cause of grief, a kind of grief which Paul finds inappropriate. Some members of the Thessalonian community have met with physical death, and the first section, 4.13–18, considers an appropriate reaction to their decease. Part of Paul's response is marked out by 4.14: 'We believe that Jesus died and rose again; so too will God bring those who died as Christians to be with Jesus' (REB).

The question is more than that of grief over the deceased. It is a question of the deceased being disadvantaged; a view which Paul strongly denies.'Those of us who are still alive will have no advantage over those who have died' (4.15). In fact the deceased in Christ will rise first; then those who are still alive will join them (4.16d–17a). So Paul concludes: 'And hence we shall always be with the Lord' and can 'counsel each other' (4.17c–18a). The conclusion is interesting especially because of the word 'always'. The argument would have led us to expect 'all' – all, both those dead and those still alive. Paul however chooses in 4.18 to emphasize 'always'. At the end of the parallel section in 5.1 his emphasis is on 'living together with him'. Continuity and togetherness are both important for him, and neither is ultimately affected by death.

So far, the REB translation gives us a relatively uncontroversial picture of the two passages. When we turn to what is specific to each of the sections we are faced with major divisions of opinion. What is clear and generally agreed is that in 4.13–18 Paul is dealing with an issue deeper than bereavement only. But what is the deeper issue? Many argue that bereavement was sharpened for the Thessalonians because they feared that those who had died would miss out on the enjoyment of the Lord's presence at the parousia, and they would miss out on that moment because only those who are alive then can share in it. The first part of that hypothesis could be right, even if the second is probaly not. There are many reasons why the Thessalonians might have feared for their dead.

The section 4.13–18 begins: *We wish you not to remain ignorant, friends about those who sleep in death; you should not grieve like the rest of mankind, who have no hope* (4.13). There is an area here not fully understood by (some of) the Thessalonians; it concerns the deceased of their number; and Paul warns against inappropriate grief. The difficulty lies in the phrase: 'like the rest of humankind'. Does that qualify the basis for grief, or the character of the grief? The Thessalonians might be grieving because they were ignorant of the Risen Son's power to deliver. But according to 1 Thess. 1.10 that was not the case. The Thessalonians might be grieving because they were ignorant of the link between resurrection and parousia. But if Paul's intention is to draw together resurrection and parousia in 1 Thess. 4, and if, as we have argued, 2 Thessalonians is Pauline and post-1 Thessalonians, then the absence of resurrection teaching in 2 Thessalonians when the parousia is a key theme is inexplicable. Some more specific point of ignorance is required. For example, the basis of grief could be if the Thessalonians were ignorant of or uncertain about God's ability to bring the dead from their apparent disadvantage into a share in continuous company with Christ. They were like the rest of humanity in that respect: 'like the rest of mankind, who have no hope'. We shall see that this is a possible solution (Barclay, 2003, pp. 151–2).

Paul's argument could, however, be that the quality of grief was inappropriate; it was the kind of inordinate grief commonly practised in the ancient world: not like the rest of humanity, in that sense. But why should it have been inordinate? Bereavement is traumatic for anyone; but perhaps the trauma was deepened by local mockery – although that does not appear likely in this section; it could be that death in their fellowship seemed a prodigy (Nicholl, pp. 75–8), warning of the End, or of wrath to come. That death might have betokened fearsome possibilities is quite possible – although that it betokened the End or wrath to come is unlikely in view of 1 Thess. 1.10 (see the commentary there). All in all, 4.13 could concern either the basis or the quality of grief, or possibly both. If the decision has to be one or the other, the basis of grief may be preferred.

What points to a specific area of ignorance or uncertainty is 4.14: For if *we believe that Jesus died and rose again . . .* then *so too will God bring those who died as Christians to be with Jesus.* The picture of God's action here resembles that in the Psalms of Solomon 18.6 and 17.23–42 (see also Isa. 11.11; 43.6), where God brings his Son, the Messiah-king (hitherto hidden until the time of God's choosing), with all his holy ones to be a blessing to Israel. But the Greek text of 4.14 specifies the continuing relationship of the deceased to Jesus. It reads: 'those asleep through Jesus', and makes the point of blessing to be where God brings them in companionship with him (that is, Jesus).

This we tell you as a word from the Lord (4.15a). 'A word of the Lord' could point us to the teaching of Jesus, an oracle of the Risen Lord, an interpretation of Scripture, or a mixture of some or all of these.

The reference of 'This' could be to 4.14b or to something which follows in 4.15b–16. Unfortunately, neither the source nor the reference is certain. Perhaps the most likely solution is that 4.15a refers back to 4.14, and designates 4.14 as a word of the Lord because it is an authoritative interpretation of a messianic tradition. Some scholars prefer to regard 'the word of the Lord' as, at least in some degree, a reference to the teaching of Jesus, and argue that 5.2 and 5.3b are similarly 'Jesus sayings' (Kim). The latter argument depending on two metaphors is probably unreliable. If 'This' refers back to the previous verse, the closest approximations to 4.14 in the Gospels are Mark 13.27 and Matt. 24.31. Certainly Mark 13.27 could only be considered in a developed forms with at least four significant additions.The suggestion above that we begin with an authoritative interpretation of a messianic tradition might be a better option. If 'This' is seen as a reference to 4.15 then we are looking for a source which gives some advantage to the dead: *those of us who are still alive when the Lord comes will have no advantage over those who have died, when the command is given, when the archangel's voice is heard, when God's trumpet sounds, then the Lord himself will descend from heaven; first the Christian dead will rise, then we who are still alive shall join them* (4.15b–17a; see 1 Thess. 1.10). In terms of the advantage of the dead, the closest approximation to 4.15 would be the reference to the survivors in 2 Esd. 13.21–34; the survivors are those who are spared to enjoy the messianic prospects because of their faithfulness, and 'the peaceable multitude' to be returned from the Diaspora for the messianic age. But the relatively late date of 2 Esdras means that we should have to find an earlier unknown source behind 2 Esdras. In terms of the threefold signal, no source has all three; the martial call is given in the Matthean tradition with the symbolic trumpet call (24.31); the picturesque parallel in Matt. 25.1–13 has only the vocal cry; the archangel's call may have a place in 2 Thess. 2.7 based on the Daniel tradition. An Old Testament passage where the great trumpet sounds to initiate the return of the children of Israel to Jerusalem, has some close parallels with 1 Thess. 4.16–18. At the end of the Isa. 16.19a the Septuagint could be read: 'the dead will rise, and (then) those living on earth will rejoice' (with 26.19b distinguishing between healing for them as against disaster for the impious). In other Greek texts of Isa. 28.19b the second group are identified as 'the sleepers who will be woken', and various other verbs are linked with the third group. At the very least Isa. 26.19 could provide the contrast between the dead (those asleep) and the living, with a clear sequence: first the dead, then the living. The argument may favour the view that 'This' in 4.15b looks back to 4.14, and in that case 4.15–16 should be translated: 'This [see 4.14] we tell you as a word from the Lord, because those of us who are still alive . . . will by no means have the advantage over those who are asleep, because the Lord himself will descend from heaven when the command is given.' The development of 1 Thess. 4.16–18 may well have been influenced by a text of Isa. 26, along with other more isolated features from the Old Testament Scriptures and the Gospel traditions.

There are several other important points from 4.15–17. It is often assumed that when Paul uses the personal pronoun 'us' in 'those of us who are alive' he is prophetically announcing that he expects to be alive at the parousia, and therefore that the parousia is imminent, and is recognized by the Thessalonians to be imminent. That sequence of statements is by no means reliable. Paul needed to differentiate clearly between those who were dead and those who were alive, and to maintain that distinction at the level of the parousia. A clear way of doing so was to associate himself with the living. If Paul did not prophetically include himself among the living at the parousia, then the case for an imminent expectation is considerably weakened. It might of course be argued that Paul makes his survival to the parousia clear elsewhere. That is suggested as an interpretation of 2 Cor. 4.16—5.5; however, it is more likely that Paul there is not claiming existence up to the parousia but claiming that conformity with Christ can imply a kind of continuity which stretches across life and physical death. This raises another question of translation and interpretation in 4.15–17. Literally, 4.15 reads: 'This we tell you as a word from the Lord: because those of us who are alive, who are left over to the Parousia of the Lord will not have an advantage over those who sleep.' In 4.17 the same phrase 'those who are left over' appears again. Does it mean 'those left over', 'those who survive', 'those who survive at cost to themselves', or 'those who remain' (to continue the responsibilities of Christian service and mission)? The position of the phrase in 4.15 before the verb 'we have no advantage over those who sleep' is probably positive, implying some degree of privilege to those who 'remain', for example to carry on the proclaiming of the good news.

1 Thess. 4.17 envisages the rapture of those remaining alive on earth at the parousia: *Then we who are still alive shall join them, caught*

up in clouds to meet the Lord in the air. Rapture, in the sense of a violent snatching of human life from the earth, belongs to several contexts: so that a righteous person avoids death (see Enoch in Gen. 5.24); or, so that the righteous will not be tempted to commit evil (Wisd. 4.11); or, so that someone is transported into heaven (2 Cor. 12.4); so that the grieving family is left behind. The picture in 4.17 is mysterious: it follows in sequence after the rising of the dead, yet the living are snatched up together with the former (the Greek could even suggest simultaneously with the former). Distinctive, too, is the rapture which makes possible the joining of the messianic procession 'in the clouds' 'into the air' to meet the Lord. That distinctiveness fits the concern of the total section 4.13—5.11, allowing both dead and living to meet and be united with their Lord. It is tempting to follow the picture of God leading a messianic procession into a further stage, a stage such as the Jewish traditions envisaged, with Jerusalem as its goal. But the concluding phrase 'into the air' suggests another direction, to 'the Jerusalem above' where *we shall always be with the Lord* (4.18).

Having read the text of 4.13–18 we are left with many questions. But the most important is how the section fits where it is between the section on love 'for "the friends"' and its parallel passage in 5.1–11 on 'being children of the light'. In our survey we established various less controversial areas, one of which was the emphasis in the two parallel passages on being together always with the Lord (continuity and community). Fairly well established, too, is that they feared for those who had died that the latter would miss out on the enjoyment of the Lord's presence at the parousia. But, as we pointed out, there are many reasons why they might have given way to that fear. One is that death might have betokened fearsome possibilities as a prodigious sign of wrath to come. But in view of the Thessalonians' declaration that they awaited the coming of the Son from heaven, it might be more in keeping with the immediate and the general context to ascribe the fear to the questions about holiness and sanctification. Were those who had died ready? Had they lived a holy enough life? Surely in that respect they are at a disadvantage over against the living, who still have the opportunity and the time to take their search for holiness further. Paul's answer is to envision the meeting of dead and living together in a continual communion with their Lord. That is indeed cause for mutual counsel and comfort. The future of both dead and living is in the hands of the God who will initiate the ultimate events and of the Lord whose they all are, whether dead or alive, and will always be. We shall see how 1 Thess. 5.1–18 takes such arguments as these still further.

In 5.1 Paul again uses a heading. It could be taken from Thessalonian correspondence brought to him by Timothy, or could be Paul's way of marking out a particular topic. The topic here is 'dates and times': *About dates and times, my friends, there is no need to write to you* (5.1). In 4.9 Paul nominated the 'topos', and addressed it both in terms of principles and precepts. As we have seen, epistles of his day could nominate topics, but then deliberately avoid dealing with them. In 4.9 he chose not to do so. He has the option again here in 5.1. Perhaps here he chose to adopt both ways; he gives the appearance of dealing with 'dates and times' but actually homed in on a related but different subject. Certainly 'dates and times' was not an area which needed the further advice Paul promised in 3.11.

5.2 does give the impression that he is writing to the topic, although he says that there is no need for him to do so, because *you yourselves know perfectly well that the day of the Lord comes like a thief in the night*. The modern reader has every reason to comment that the Thessalonians may well know what Paul is writing about, but the uses of 'day of the Lord' in the prophetic literature and in the New Testament have a bewildering variety of meanings. To place this verse in that spectrum of meanings is a difficult task indeed. To this we must add, however, that there are important constants of meaning in the 'day of the Lord' references, for example Theocentric or Christocentric elements. The 'day of the Lord' means that the holiness and majesty of God are revealed and his will and purpose fulfilled. Further, that constant element carries a direct critique of the present world order. The 'day of the Lord' may refer to Christ, and where it does so the relationship of 'the day' to Christ varies in several ways. In fact in 1 Thess. 5.1–11 the role of Christ itself covers a spectrum, from the 'night thief' to the daylight in which we already belong, and from there to the end-time home for all his followers. It is probably this spectrum of meanings within 1 Thess. 5.1–12 which assisted the misunderstandings following the false alarm in 2 Thess. 2.2. How Paul deals with that confusion is to sketch out that both the present and ongoing world order must still await that final act of Christ (2 Thess. 2.8). The thief tradition, too, passed through many stages, and again it is not entirely clear where 1 Thess. 5.2 fits into that story. At an early stage its focus was the suddenness and unexpectedness of the thief's coming; it became linked to the Gospel Son of Man tradition, so that the suddenness of the thief's arrival and that of the Son of Man were compared. In Rev. 3.3 and 16.15 it presented a warning to the faithful of judgement; and in 2 Pet. 3.10 on the 'day of the Lord' the faithful find security in the Saviour Christ. 1 Thess. 5.2 probably belongs to an early stage, except that the addition, the thief *in the night,* is part of the argument in 1 Thess. 5.1–11, and may be Paul's adaptation of the picture. 5.2 pictures the 'night thief' and 5.4 comments: 'For you, my friends, do not live in the dark, for the day to catch you unawares like a thief' (Nicholls, p. 53).

The part played by 5.3 in that argument has been variously described. Some regard it as a warning of judgement; others contrast the 'day of the Lord' directly with the Roman peace propaganda of the early Empire; others recollect Jeremiah's attack on the false prophets who cry 'Peace' where there is no peace (see Jer. 6.14 'All is well!'). A preferable alternative is to treat 5.3 as proverbial, without any one specific historical reference. Like a proverb the verse contains present tenses: 'When people say *"All is peaceful, all is secure",* then, sudden at their door, is *destruction,* sudden *as the pangs that come on a woman in childbirth; and* they will not *escape.'* Those lured into a false sense of security face disaster from which they are unable to escape. Luke 21.34–36 has similar vocabulary; the language in Luke forms a warning to avoid 'dissipation, drunkenness and wordly cares' so as to be awake at 'the day' and to be able to escape and stand before the Son of Man. Paul is making a similar point in 1 Thess. 5.4, except that he is quite clear that the Thessalonians have no need to be in a danger from which there is no escape. The same point will be made in 2 Thess. 1.2–12 where the Thessalonians do not need to fear the 'day of the Lord'; the *'olethros'* (the ruin, or destruction) is for the persecutors and the disobedient. *But you, my friends, are not in the dark,* for *the day to* catch *you,* as a (night-)thief might, unawares (5.4). The movement of thought here in 1 Thess. 5.3–5 is very close to Ephesians 5: 'Though you once were darkness, now as Christians you are light. Prove yourselves at home in the light, for where light is, there is a harvest of goodness, righteousness and truth' and 'whatever is exposed to the light itself becomes light. That is why it is said: "Awake, sleeper, rise from the dead, and Christ will shine upon you"' (Eph. 5.8–9, 13b–14). Just so is Paul's movement of thought. He moves in 1 Thess. 5.2–5 from the danger of being caught unawares by the day of the Lord, as by a night-thief, to the entirely different circumstances in which the converts now live; they live now in the light. 'For *you are all*, all of you, *children of light, children of day*.' The expression 'children of day' picks up the opening topic of 'the day of the Lord', and asserts that the Thessalonians belong to the day. What God has done in Christ has transformed the Thessalonians, their patterns of faith, love and hope (see 5.8). They live in the light; and he associates himself and his colleagues with that transformation: *We do not belong to night and darkness* (5.5b). So having begun with the opening topic of the 'day of the Lord' Paul has moved to the daylight of Christ in which they all, Paul, his colleagues and the converts now live. He has moved from the question of dates and times, about when the 'day of the Lord' is to come, and which they are perfectly well aware cannot be known in advance, to what they most certainly know of their present circumstances and what those circumstances signify for the present and for the future. He is now ready to draw his conclusion.

In 5.6 Paul begins with words which mark the start of his conclusions: 'So then, what are we to conclude?' *We must not sleep like the rest, but keep awake and sober.* With the privilege of these changed circumstances – chosen by God, sanctified by the Spirit, living in Christ – there are obvious responsibilities. Since we live in the daylight, our behaviour must reflect the daylight; or, as Paul continues: for *sleepers sleep at night and drunkards get drunk at night, but we, who belong to the day, must keep sober* (5.7–8a). Having reached the key conclusion, and used these powerful pictures to describe the changed circumstances in which Christians live, he must now translate those pictures into the realities of the everyday. To do so he draws on a passage from Isaiah which over generations inspired God's people. Originally Isaiah 59 set out God's preparations for a 'day of the Lord' when he dealt with his people's wickedness, injustice and deceit, which had raised a barrier between himself and his chosen ones (59.2). It was as if, says the prophet, we look for light, but all is darkness, for daybreak, but we must walk in deep gloom (59.9). When the Lord saw this he was displeased (59.15); he put on righteousness as a breastplate, and salvation as a helmet on the head; he put on the garments of vengeance and wrapped zeal about him like a cloak (59.17). So from the west the Lord's name will be feared and his glory revealed from the rising of the sun (59.19). 'He will come as a Redeemer to Zion This is the word of the Lord' (59.20). 'My spirit which rests on you and my words which I have put into your mouth will never fail you from generation to generation' (59.21). That passage inspired the writer of the Wisdom of Solomon 5.18, and of Ephesians 6.14–18. It is difficult to estimate how far the passage influenced Paul in his writing of 1 Thessalonians. But what we can say with certainty is that in 1 Thess. 5.8 Paul rewrites Isaiah 59 in the spirit of the triad with which Paul began the letter: *be sober*, since you have put on *the breastplate of faith and love, and hope of salvation for a helmet* (1 Thess. 5.8). The circumstances which Paul depicted in 1 Thess. 1.1–10, the original events at Thessalonica, are now described by Paul as the equipment which they all already possess to fulfil their responsibilities. This is what he means by 'being sober', by 'living in the daylight'. Whether it was the Isaiah 59 passage, or Paul's reference to 'salvation' as a helmet, or the recollection of the Thessalonian event, we cannot be sure; but some connecting link led Paul from the triad with which he began – faith, love and hope – to the ultimate reason why we should 'be sober': because *God has not destined us for* wrath, *but for the full attainment of salvation through our Lord Jesus Christ who died for us* (5.9–10a). God's election, attainment of salvation through Jesus Christ, participation in him – all are brought together in a single verse (see Introduction, section 10), as the basis for our being in the daylight and the reason and motivation for our living according to the daylight. Then, to expound further what is involved in the attainment of salvation, Paul adds: this is in order that *awake or asleep we might live* together *in company with him* (5.10b). The reference of the metaphors 'sleeping' and 'waking' shifts. The work of salvation concerns the living (those awake) and those who are dead (those asleep) and brings both into the continuous companionship of being with Christ. Those who have died with Christ in the sense of participating in the here and now in Christ's death, through death to self, disobedience and the structures of humanity's self-imprisonment, whether they are still physically alive or whether they belong to 'the dead in Christ' (4.16; and here Paul assumes the argumentation of 4.13–18), they share the same promise at the parousia (the 'day of the Lord') of a continuing life with Christ. That is a promise offering mutual consolation: *Therefore encourage one another, build one another up – as indeed you do* (5.11). The motif of 'building one another up' is picked up in a number of ways in the concluding verses of the chapter.

There are several comments to make at this point in the commentary. The first is that the twin concerns of the prayer in

3.12–13 are carried through the whole of 1 Thess. 4.1—5.11.'Love of the "friends"' and 'the hope of being blameless in holiness through Christ at the parousia' give a coherence to the second part of 1 Thessalonians, and they belong closely together in the affirmations of 'living together in the continuing company of Christ'.

That leads to a second comment. The mutual love and building up of one another may well have another range of relevance for the hearers (5.27). The first part of 1 Thessalonians had a focus upon the 'Thessalonica event', and that event directly concerned Gentile converts (1.8–10) and those with whom Paul's style of living as a manual labourer resonated. The second part of 1 Thessalonians has occasional references back to that event, but the concentration in 4.1—5.11 on Judaeo-Christian principles, precepts, motifs and exegesis suggests another context. Paul's theme of 'love for the "friends"' looks to the coexistence and cooperation of both Gentile converts and Jewish converts. The letter is to be read to all of them, and is intended for all of them.

A third comment picks up the greater expertise to be expected of the Jewish Christians in Thessalonica in the interpretation of Scripture. We shall find this reflected in 2 Thessalonians also. It is hardly possible that the implications of the phrase the 'day of the Lord' would have been gathered in the same way by Gentiles and Jews, unless of course some of the Gentiles were long-standing converts to Judaism (the God-fearers); and even for them an extensive acquaintance with Scripture cannot be assumed. If Jewish Christians were aware of the emphases and subtleties of Paul's argument, they might well have come away from the joint hearing of the letter wondering whether Paul was claiming that the 'day of the Lord' was both here and still to come. That could be a reason for immediate acceptance of the rumour exposed in 2 Thess. 2.2.

The fourth comment also concerns a possible area of misunderstanding in the second half of 1 Thessalonians. Cleverly, Paul plays on the possibilities offered by the contrast between 'sleeping' and 'being awake'. In the setting of 'night and day' the contrast offers a physical interpretation, in the setting of 'light and dark' a moral metaphor, and in the setting of life and death a way of understanding the Christian present experience and future hope. Unfortunately in 5.10 a less perceptive convert might well confuse the 'life/death' contrast with the moral 'light/dark' contrast. Anyone who has written a letter or e-mail and realized after sending it that there was a seriously ambiguous phrase within it will understand if Paul chose to try to correct the error as soon as he could.

Final instructions
5.12–22

Leadership among the Thessalonian followers of Christ is defined only by quality and function. No names are mentioned, and no continuity of responsibility is affirmed. Relative anonymity could have given leadership some protection in the neighbourhood quarrels. In these respects there are similarities with the trade associations; as there are in the terms used of leadership. If there were distinct groups among the converts in Thessalonica, leadership could well have been an area of friction. So Paul addresses the attitudes appropriate to leaders whoever they may be. Where functions define leadership, particularly in communities where the gifts of the Holy Spirit are understood to be the experience of all the members, the overlap of activities between leadership and members could be a further area of friction. Once again the experience of trade associations where all possessed some skills could have provided patterns for 'good practice'. Recognition of services rendered offers a starting point for Paul. *We beg you, friends, to acknowledge those who are working so hard among you* (5.12). The phrase 'working hard' has resonances with the expressions of the triad in 1 Thess. 1.3, and relates specifically to work within the Christian fellowship. As those who live out 'love of the "friends"' they offer an example to be followed; so acknowledgement of their work includes recognition of the community style they represent. The leaders, rather than enabling people to find a community that suits membership needs, may well need to instantiate the more fundamental principle that has a universal claim to attract and to hold. Paul refers to these hard workers also as '*leaders* in the Lord'. Here the parallel with ancient voluntary associations is less helpful. The communities they serve by their labour acknowledge primarily the Jesus Christ who is deliverer and Lord. Perhaps Paul has in mind the way in which his own ministry has been formed in that context, so that the pictures of 'nurse's self-offering' and 'fatherly, personal attention' have become appropriate in his case, and might well be so for the leaders present in the city. In the Greek text 'in the Lord' qualifies leadership alone, and that would add weight to the view that leadership needs to be shaped in the distinctively Christian way. The description '*counsellors*' places them in the structure of paternal care, and corresponds to the task of helping community members to move forward to new and expanding ways of expressing 'love of the "friends"'. 'To counsel' in the Greek text is particularly appropriate to advancing others in moral development. That has, however, to be exercised within a structure shaped by mutuality of counselling, and also by inter-change of roles between leaders and members. If that is correct, Paul bequeathed to the Thessalonian Christians one of the most difficult kinds of leadership, and it is one which depends to a great extent on the respect, affection, patience and understanding of the membership. Only the willingness of the membership to work har-moniously together and with their leaders makes it feasible. Little wonder that Paul adds: *Hold them in the highest esteem and affection for the work they do. Live at peace among yourselves.*

1 Thess. 5.14 could be an exhortation to leaders; but there is no reason to think that the leaders formed a defined group with a precise and continuing remit; nor is there evidence of a change of address between 5.14 and 5.15–16 (Best, p. 229). It is much more likely that this sentence is to be addressed to everyone. *We urge you, friends, to rebuke the idle, encourage the faint-hearted, support the weak, and be patient with everyone.* The first group are *'ataktoi'* (REB 'the idle'); they could be people who are lazy or people who do not work for some good reason or other. Their existence could be a reason for Paul in 4.11 to advise converts to do manual labour, as Paul himself does; and 2 Thess. 3.11 uses a related form of the same word along-side the phrase 'doing no work'. On the other hand a form related to *'ataktoi'* is also used in 2 Thess. 3.6, and there the translation 'behaving idly' would sound distinctly odd; also, there are Greek words for 'idle' which do not appear in the Thessalonian correspon-dence, whereas *'ataktoi'* literally means 'indisciplined', 'disorderly'. 'Disorderly' would make good sense in 5.14, and in both passages in 2 Thess. 3. The voluntary associations had to make provision for such members, members who were undisciplined, or whose work was unsatisfactory. A Christian community in Thessalonica could well have modelled their procedures on the same system. Paul says they should be rebuked. It used to be thought that some Christians in Thessalonica did not work because they thought of the 'day of the Lord' as too close to make work worthwhile. But at no point in the discussions of this group does Paul imply such a motivation; he simply says (in 1 Thessalonians) they should be 'rebuked'. The sec-ond group are 'the faint-hearted' or 'the anxious'. The main biblical evidence for the word is in the Septuagint. An example would be: 'Brace the arms that are limp, steady the knees that give way; say

to the anxious, "Be strong, fear not! Your God comes to save you
. . . "'(Isa. 35.4). According to Paul they need consolation or encouragement (one of the tasks of a father, see 2.12). Of the third group,
'the weak', Paul uses a verb indicating 'give personal attention to',
'give pastoral care to', 'be there to help'. In other Pauline letters the
contexts might suggest that 'the weak' are morally susceptible, or
over-scrupulous, or weak in faith. But the context in 5.14 does little
to help us to that extent. We have to rely on Paul's choice of the verb
for a guide and on his concern in the whole epistle with mutuality: be there when people need you! The final group is inclusive of
everyone, perhaps those who might think they do not belong to any
of the first three, but nevertheless need to be dealt with patiently.
That would make good sense here. The verb 'be patient with' is the
richest of all the four imperative verbs in this verse. Although it is
found in everyday contexts, in Paul it can reflect the nature and
work of God (Exod. 34.6). 'Patience' can therefore take on aspects
of firmness, and long-term vision and action; it recognizes how
God deals with humanity in its self-imprisonment. It is the space
given to us by God in which we recognize our shortcomings and
that they do not belong in the divine order (Wisd. 15.1–5).The use
of 'be patient' in 5.14 is therefore a Pauline challenge to any group
of Christians. As in the advice to 'Live in peace' (5.13) it designates
the discovery of a whole way of relating to others. One might call
it the first bridgehead in the operation to deal with the world's
chaos.That is how Paul sees God's work; and to use the verb of
our responsibilities to each other is to reveal pastoral care in all its
amazing possibilities.

The connection with 5.15 is clear. If we are to be patient at that
level of understanding human nature, then retaliation needs to give
way to seeking the long-term benefit of all, Christians and non-
Christians alike, and to acting accordingly: *See to it that no one pays
back wrong for wrong, but always aim at what is best for each other and
for all*. The theme of 'love for the "friends"' is taken in this precept
to a new level with 1 Thessalonians, and seen as a model by which
the benefit of every human being can be sought. Nevertheless, the
first half of the precept is stated in what seems to be a limited way:
evil is not to be repaid with evil. That is at least a stage beyond
'if one repays evil for good, evil will never leave his house' (Prov.
17.13). Some Jewish precepts use the limited form and balance it
with the need to show charity. The precepts of Tobit given to Tobias
occupy that position; they have the negative form: 'do not do to

others what you yourself hate', but they link that form, as 1 Thess. 5.15b does, to a more charitable provision (Tobit 4.15–16). 1 Thess. 5.15 is certainly a more Jewish form than we find in the Beatitudes: 'Love your enemies; do good to those who hate you; bless those who curse you; pray for those who treat you spitefully (Luke 6.27–28). The main question in 1 Thess. 5 is why, if Paul knows the more positive forms, he does not always use them. Paul does use more positive forms elsewhere. Rom. 12.17–20 begins as 1 Thess. 5.15 does, with 'Never pay back evil for evil', adding 'leave revenge to God'; and then continues: 'But there is another text' (more positive than Tobit because it includes the enemy):'if your enemy is hungry feed him . . . Do not let evil conquer you, but use good to conquer evil.' The 'command to love' has already been used (Rom. 12.9–10). 1 Peter also balances 'Do not repay wrong with wrong' with 'respond with blessing', 'for a blessing is what God intends you to receive' (1 Pet. 3.8). So why does 1 Thess. 5.15a use only the limited form? Part of the answer is probably that Paul's main intention in 5.15 is to commend, as he did in the prayer-wish in 3.12, concern for the outsider. The letter has been so full of the need for mutuality that the danger of the community, under threat, closing on itself is very real. So, limited though 5.15 may be, in that it does not move on to the theme of good conquering evil, it does establish the universal responsibility of Christians; as indeed should be the case, in view of the work of Christ which opens up the restoration of humanity for all (5.10). Paul may not use the theme of good conquering evil, but in 5.15b he does use the corrective 'but', and then commends unceasing pursuit of the good not only for one another but for all.

There are Pauline parallels to the sequence of commands in 5.16–22, notably in Romans 12. But, as in 5.15, Paul is addressing the Thessalonian needs with care. *Always be joyful; pray continually; give thanks whatever happens* (5.16–18a). The initial cluster – joy, prayer, thanksgiving – appears in 1.1–10 as Paul involves his readers in reflection on the Thessalonian event, and they are used together before the conclusion to the first part of the letter (3.9–10), as Paul makes a response to Timothy's good news. The adverbs too in 5.17–18 recall the opening of the epistle: Paul's thanksgiving and prayer may have as their focus the Thessalonica event but both are continual and constant. The difference between 5.16–18 and these other contexts is that the verbs are imperatives and the adverbs play a somewhat different role. The references to joy in the epistle have already been noted in the commentary on 3.9b, and their combination makes possible that deeper joy which like a reservoir should continually be available in times of emergency and daily need. Modern Christian communities, notably those in Eastern Europe, have rediscovered those resources. *'Always be joyful'* has been a genuine consolation. The 'adverb' *continually* in 5.17 has so far been associated with thankful recollection (as it will again in Rom. 1.8). It is one form of prayer among many which belong to the pilgrimage delineated in the prayer-wish of 3.12–13. In particular, there is the need for intercessory prayer as a mutual responsibility. Paul is about to remind them of this (5.25). *'Whatever happens'* expands thanksgiving beyond particular times and occasions: *for this is what God wills for you in Christ Jesus* (15.18). The REB is taking 5.18b as a reference back to 5.18a (see the comma between the two parts): thanksgiving whatever happens is (or, joyfulness, prayer and thanksgiving are) God's will for you. A possible reason for taking 5.18b with what follows rather than with what precedes is the occurrence of the same phrase in 4.3; there 'This' points forward: this is the will of God, that you should be holy. Both readings of 5.18 are possible, either retrospective or prospective. If it is retrospective, 'this' refers to thanksgiving, and 'for' explains why thanksgiving is so important. If it is prospective, 'this' refers to 'not quenching the Spirit', and 'for' explains that thanksgiving is always appropriate, even when a Spirit-event is unwelcome. The decision between the two, retrospective or prospective, is not an easy one: thanksgiving and not quenching the Spirit (especially in view of 4.3–8) are both possible reference points. Slightly more appropriate, however, is the retrospective reference because of the phrase 'in Christ Jesus'. It is slightly easier to assume that thanksgiving is God's will 'in Christ Jesus' than that 'Quench not the Spirit' is God's will 'in Christ Jesus'. In a fully Trinitarian pattern of thought the latter might be preferable, but that cannot be claimed for 1 Thessalonians. The decision is a tight one, particularly if one imagines Timothy bringing information about Thessalonian debates on prophecy (as 5.19–20 suggest). The retrospective approach has a major advantage: it provides an excellent link between 5.16–17 and 5.19–20. Indeed, it provides a continuity across 5.16–22 under the theme of public worship. It remains to decide how far 5.18b refers back: to 5.18a only, to 5.16–17, or as far as 5.13.

It is difficult for us to measure the importance of the expansion of thanksgiving to 'every occasion'. The Greek word *'eucharisto'* has today, through its association with the Lord's Supper, taken on an all-embracing reference. The Lord's Supper, with its 'Great Thanksgiving' recapitulating all that God in Christ has done for us, and with its summoning of the Spirit, can be aptly named today the 'Eucharist par excellence', a thanksgiving appropriate for every season and time and place. The situation in Paul's day was undoubtedly different. We know nothing of Paul's teaching on the Lord's Supper to the Thessalonians, as we know nothing of his teaching there on Baptism. It is, as we have said, hard to think that either Lord's Supper or Baptism was missing from his initial work there. We might, however, recall that at the time Paul and his colleagues were shaping 1 Thessalonians they were also working in Corinth. There, to judge by 1 Cor. 11.23, Paul was already passing on to the Corinthians the tradition of the Lord's own Supper with its focus on thanksgiving, salvation and sharing (Thiselton, p. 864). Although the centuries have opened up for us profound experiences in the Eucharist, it could nevertheless have been the case in Paul's day that 'thanksgiving' had a rich enough profile to be designated 'God's will in Christ Jesus'.

We have noted that common to both 5.18b and 4.3 is the designation: 'This is God's will for you.' Is there a link between the two passages? 5.16–18 enable us to see joy, prayer, and thanksgiving as features of Thessalonian worship, and worship as a possible overall theme across at least 5.16–22. The interrelationship of the three elements of 5.16–17 in other parts of the letter, and the adverbs used in each of the three, make a strong case for worship not only as a continuity in 5.16–18, but as a major theme at the conclusion of the letter. It may provide continuity even perhaps from 5.13 to 5.22, and one with links with 5.23, which offers a prayer-wish for God's gift of holiness. Is that perhaps the connecting link between 5.16–17 and 4.3? Worship is an integral part of the Pauline letter. Although expressed in epistolary form, the realities of worship cannot be excluded from the background to the letter and from its effectiveness as communication. Holiness, as we have seen, has been a constant refrain in the thanksgivings and prayer-wishes. Now we discover worship and holiness to be the two areas designated as 'This is the will of God for you'. The association between them is evident in 5.23, providing a continuity across 5.13–23 – a significant concluding section for the whole letter (Standaert, p. 183).

A 'quenching of the Spirit' (5.19; the REB has *Do not stifle inspiration*) would hardly be possible if it concerned the life of the whole Church. The only circumstances in which we could imagine that happening would be fostered by a major split within the Church. In Thessalonica the Spirit played a significant part in the initial event according to the mutual memory of the participants. Had other groups, for example those converted in other contexts, failed to share in the life of the Spirit, or in the life of the Spirit as experienced in the Thessalonica event, then possibly 5.19 might address a general problem. But there is no real evidence of such a split. Different though the backgrounds of the Christian groups there may have been, 1 Thessalonians encourages a picture where 'love of the "friends"' is realized and could be even further advanced. Much more likely is that in the context of worship some difficulty or other arose which called for guidance from Paul and his colleagues. The worship link between 5.18 and 5.19–23 recalled a thanksgiving by a prophet or some other utterance in worship which needed attention: Do not *despise prophetic utterances* (5.19), Paul advises them.

These verses are so succinct that it is impossible to find sufficient detail in the text to know for sure what Paul was saying. All we can do is to recall that he was working in Corinth at the time he wrote 1 Thessalonians, and that gifts of the Spirit there called for perceptive pastoral attention in letters he thereafter wrote to Corinth. That is unsatisfactory as a guide to 1 Thessalonians in at least two respects: we know how different the situations in Thessalonica and Corinth were, and we do not know by what stages Paul's thoughts in Corinth matured in the pastoral advice he finally committed to writing in 1 and 2 Corinthians. Nevertheless, it is helpful to see how Paul understood prophetic utterances at those later stages, in the hope that we can see what 1 Thess. 5.19–22 might have meant.

In the Pauline tradition, prophecy operates within the life of the community, and at least some of its utterances will belong in a context which can be termed worship (1 Thess. 5.16–18). The descriptions of prophecy underline that function. Prophecy, according to recent studies is a gift of the Holy Spirit, combines pastoral insight into the needs of persons, communities and situations with the ability to address these with a God-given utterance (whether unprompted or prepared), leading to challenge or comfort, judgement or consolation, but ultimately building up the whole community. A model for defining 'building up' would be Paul's own ministry, where exhortation connotes a sense parallel with gospel proclamation (1 Thess. 2.2–3), and where comfort takes the form of pastoral care (1 Thess. 2.14–15). To *despise* such *prophetic utterances* (1 Thess. 5.20) would be folly. Mistakes can be made in prophecy and therefore prophecy needs to be weighed and tested (1 Thess. 5.21a: *test them all*; for refusal to test the prophets, see Didache 11.7). How may they be tested? The role of Scripture and a sense of the coherence of the insights of the Spirit would be part of the bedrock against which prophecy could be tested (1 Thess. 5.21b: *keep hold of what is good*). Similarly, the Spirit's concern is for order as against chaos, and this may require of prophets regard to the effects of socially unacceptable confrontations (1 Thess. 5.22: *avoid all forms of evil*). The mind can operate as a check on inordinate zeal, and the mind's productivity in the service of others is a further test of prophecy's value. Danger attends prophecy where it serves self-enhancement (see 5.22 again). Although prophecy does not belong to an office, it can be productive of leadership (see 5.12). It has a place within the tradition of proclaiming the gospel of Christ (Thiselton, pp. 956–1168).

The final prayer-wish
5.23–24

The final prayer-wish picks up two of the key features of the preceding verses: *May God himself, the God of peace, make you holy through and through* (5.23). Aspects of peace have ranged in the preceding verses from the work of leaders, to the attitudes of members, from the mutual understanding to personal wholeness, from prophetic order to the building up of the community. As the Spirit stands for order against chaos, so God stands for peace over against discord. Perhaps the central aspect of 'peace' in the letter is the answering and allaying of anxieties, especially the anxiety concerned with the community's standing before God and standing at the parousia before God. The prayer for holiness expounds holiness in its fullest range: Make you holy through and through, *and* may your *spirit* be kept *sound*, and your *soul and body, blamelessly* at the parousia of *our Lord Jesus Christ* (5.23). The prayer-wish has caused comment especially because of its apparent tripartite or trichotomic division of the human being. We shall argue that Paul does not choose the terms because he has a particular fixed view of how a human being is made up (a fixed view is not deducible from the complex patterns of language which he uses in his letters) or how human existence can properly be understood (existential approaches to his language have proved equally open to doubt).

He chooses the terms in 1 Thessalonians because they represent three ways in which the approach to holiness before God might be understandable. The word 'spirit' ('*pneuma*') in 5.23 stands apart from the other two, '*psuche*' and '*soma*'. 'Spirit' alone has before it the emphatic adjective 'sound'. In 1 Thessalonians all the uses of 'spirit' (except for 5.23), whether or not accompanied with 'holy', refer to the Holy Spirit. Some scholars have argued that to use 'spirit' of a human being in the context of references to God as Holy Spirit is to see God standing over against humanity. But even in its human references 'spirit' is always holy in the Pauline letters. In this he agrees with Hellenistic Judaism; as in the work of the Jewish philosopher Philo '*pneuma*' constitutes a link between humanity and God. It marks a kinship by virtue of which humanity is transcendent, holy and made in the divine image. It marks openness to the transcendental life of God. In 1 Cor. 2.6–16 there is an analogy between the human spirit and the divine spirit, and the analogy is dependent on their relatedness (Isaacs, p. 80). Among the complex patterns of Paul's usage for the human being there are other words which might be considered, at some level or other, as interchangeable with '*pneuma*'; the word '*nous*' (mind) for example. But none of them carries that link with the Holy Spirit's work which characterizes 1 Thessalonians.

So the first term in 5.23, slightly set apart from the others in the Greek text, is for all the Thessalonians, so Paul prays, to be kept 'sound' 'complete' 'undamaged' at the parousia. How Paul saw the relationship between the members of the community and the Spirit of God at work among them is nowhere explained in 1 Thessalonians. Elsewhere in Paul the gifts of the Spirit and unity in the Spirit give us part of the answer. What Paul is praying in 5.23 concerns the whole community of Christ. Their 'spirit' is assurance for them all of their safe protection by the Holy Spirit. The second term, '*psuche*', translated by the REB 'soul', is differently used in biblical literature. Its association with the living breath breathed into Adam at creation illustrates one of use. It is used by Paul of the living being in its social and political contexts (see Rom. 13.1). It is the living being as it carries responsibility, as it belongs within the pattern of human living, and possesses the potential we have as living beings, either in maintaining life or being able and willing to sacrifice its life. In 1 Thess. 2.8, following the illustration of the proverbial nurse, the term is used of the lives which Paul and his colleagues would gladly have 'gifted' for the converts. Rather than 'soul', which in other contexts it could mean, Paul may have in mind the living being in all its structures and potential, which we have seen need to be shaped by the attitudes and responses designated 'holy'.

The third term, 'body', is one of the most discussed terms in the study of Pauline literature, and there is little agreement yet as to what it is in Paul's writings that a human being has which can properly be called 'body'. Undoubtedly there are Pauline uses which carry physical (as well as emotional and psychological) implications. 1 Cor. 7.4 is a classic case. In 1 Thess. 4.3 God's will, as holiness, requires 'keeping oneself away from fornication (or sexual impurity)', and what follows in 1 Thess. 4.4 (leaving aside our discussion of 4.6) leaves no doubt that holiness concerns the use of what one physically possesses. At this point the question arises of what Paul means in the prayer by: may it be kept blamelessly at the parousia of the Lord Jesus Christ. Had the text read 'until the parousia' there would have been little cause for surprise. But the phrase 'at the parousia' is thought-provoking. We might, however, reflect that earlier in 1 Thessalonians Paul had introduced the subject of 'reward' at the parousia (2.18–20); and in 2 Cor. 5.10 'before the tribunal of Christ' 'each must receive what is due to him for his conduct in the body, good or bad'. The 'body' is by no means irrelevant at the parousia, according to Paul; as in the case of Paul's work of ministry, what is done in the body carries with it reward or loss, though by no means necessarily loss of salvation (1 Cor. 4.13–17). Paul's prayer-wish for their safe arrival at the parousia takes note of all those features of the pilgrimage in holiness. It also leaves the final act of sanctification to God: 'Now may the God of peace sanctify you through and through.' That is an ultimate bastion again Thessalonian anxiety. For '*He who calls you keeps faith; he will do it*' (5.24; see Introduction, section 10). What is implied in God 'keeping faith with us' overarches all our experiences and the disobedience, selfishness and chaos in the world. That was made clear in the earlier discussions of 'wrath' and the 'fate of Israel':

> Whatever the changes and loss of our temporal experience, God carries them too within his own relationship with us, and redeems them: God is faithful. A call to faithfulness follows for us. It is a universal call. It will fulfil human identity and the human condition as such. We all need to be faithful and trustworthy in all ways possible in our fallen and finite condition.

(For the significance of this passage for daily work and industry, see White, p. 150)

A *request for intercession*
5.25

Paul nows asks that the mutuality evident throughout the letter may be shown in the Thessalonians' intercession for Paul and his colleagues: *Friends, pray for us also* (5.25). This is repeated in 2 Thess. 3.1–3 where the situation, presumably in Corinth, gives Paul considerable pain.

The kiss of peace
5.26

On behalf of Paul and his colleagues, since Timothy alone was able to visit, he asks that they *greet all our fellow-Christians with the kiss of peace* (5.26). This sharing of peace on behalf of absent friends indicates a fresh reality to the earlier prayer to the God of peace (5.23). The 'kiss of peace' in fact underlined and nurtured the mutuality, reciprocity and oneness of status and identity, which all Christians share across divisions of race, class, gender and here, even of space. 1 Cor. 16.20 places together greetings from the whole community, and the greeting of one another with the kiss of peace. A kiss in public was regarded in some Graeco-Roman circles with distaste and its ambivalence and corruptibility are as ancient as they are evident. In Christian circles it became a sign of honour and respect, and, as in Acts 20.37, an expression of deep affection, loyalty and, at departures, of distress, in the case of Acts 20, because Paul might never return. The evidence from the early Church indicates the place of the kiss in eucharistic practice, but it is by no means certain that it had entered eucharistic worship in Paul's time, and even less certain that one could assume from the reference to 'the kiss of peace' that the community reading of the letter took place in a eucharistic setting. Paul refers to greeting one another with a kiss of peace in Rom. 16.16 and 2 Cor. 13.12 (see also 1 Pet. 5.14). Its position there and in 1 Thess. 5.26 could imply the way in which Paul would welcome the community to respond to each other following

79

the community reading of his letter. 1 Thess. 5.26 has the inclusive form, 'all the "friends"'; and immediately thereafter there is the strong binding of the community to the reading of the letter.

The oath concerning public reading
5.27

If the 'kiss of peace' was a form of greeting symbolic of the unity of community, the requirement in 5.27 that the letter should be read before everyone, so that everyone could share its information and enjoy the immediacy of Paul's epistolary presence, must have had the unity of the whole community as its goal: *I adjure you by the Lord to have this letter read to them all.* The same motivation stands behind Col. 4.16, where those who are to hear the letter are from communities in separate geographical centres. The public reading of a text, shared by a body of people, is an event with its own distinctive dynamics. That is particularly so when the text is from a well-known individual, and when the text is a response to conversations held previously with the community, in this case conversations with Timothy. The varied emotions and reactions expressed by listeners in the course of the reading would become part of the community's experience of the message, and are intended by Paul to contribute to the function and effectiveness of the letter. The reading of 1.1–10 would have caught the attention of those who witnessed the Thessalonica event, and they no doubt affirmed that what was read was true to their memory of the event. Those who were not present then would have been interested to hear Paul's view of what happened. When 4.1–10 was read, some would have been baffled by the detail, while others would have been glad to hear affirmed what they took to be important moral teaching. The letter would have assisted the different groups to listen to each other. Eyes would have turned to those who were not working as 5.14 was read; and the comments about those giving leadership should not, according to 5.27, have been leaked beforehand. The method Paul required would add transparency to the message. Those who wanted some answers about Paul's prolonged absence would have listened carefully to Paul's view of what had happened. As we recognize the profound effect of a letter read in community, we can understand the strength of Paul's 'I adjure'. Paul was not breaking new ground, so much as ensuring that a good tradition, that of public reading, should be used to advantage. A unifying feature of the occasion could also have been that no one heard the letter first, and those who could not read well could appreciate its contents with the literary expert. The community event would also have a significant effect – that will be important when we come to consider 2 Thessalonians; the attention given corporately by the community to the letter inevitably raised its status. However careful Paul had been (and however careful he was in the letter itself) not to claim too much weight for himself and his colleagues he could not control the intonations of the reader nor could he lower the sense of occasion felt by all. In so far as Timothy had registered correctly that the people desperately wanted to see Paul again, the emotion involved in the reading of his words would have been tangible (Oestreich, 224–45).

The grace
5.28

The end of the letter as we have it recalls the beginning: *The grace of our Lord Jesus Christ be with you!* That the opening of the letter began with the grace and peace of God our Father illustrates the balance throughout the letter between the work of the Father and the work of Jesus Christ. If the opening looks forward to the message of God's gift of peace to his people (see 5.14–23), its ending looks back to the promise of being together always with the Lord, made possible through the grace of Christ. It is for the end that the grace of Christ gives the assurance which the Thessalonians need; despite all their failings and uncertainties: Christ will be with them then as their deliverer when they need him most.

2 Thessalonians

The address
1.1

V. 1 *Paul, Silvanus, and Timothy to the church of the Thessalonians who belong to God our Father and the Lord Jesus Christ.* The three colleagues appear together again, joint auhors as in 1 Thessalonians, and, as we shall see, the letter uses the 'we' forms. Assuming that 2 Thessalonians is authentically Pauline, this would mean that the colleagues are still together. The similarity of 2 Thessalonians to 1 Thessalonians suggests that only a short space of time passed between the writing of the two letters.

The opening of 2 Thessalonians is identical with that of 1 Thessalonians, except for one small difference, the addition of 'our' before Father. It is the first of many agreements with or close similarities with 1 Thessalonians. The agreements are listed below, and similarities are given in bold type. The basis of the comparison is the REB text:

2 Thessalonians		1 Thessalonians
1.1	Paul, Silvanus, and Timothy to the church of the Thessalonians who belong to God **our** Father and the Lord Jesus Christ.	1.1
1.2	grace to you and peace	1.1c
1.3	**Friends, we are** always **bound** to thank God for you	
	faith and love	1.3
	love for **each other grows ever greater**	(3.12)
1.5	worthy of **the** kingdom **of God**	(2.12)

2 Thessalonians		1 Thessalonians
1.7	**the Lord Jesus is revealed**	
	from heaven	(1.10)
1.10	**among** all believers	1.7
1.11	**we pray for you always**	(1.2)
	calling	(1.4)
	every **act inspired by** faith	(1.3)
2.1	**the coming** of our Lord Jesus	
	and his gathering of us to	
	himself	(4.17)
2.5	**told you this while I was still**	
	with you	3.4
2.13	salvation	(5.9)
	in the Spirit **who consecrates**	
	you	(4.7–8)
2.14	call**ed** you . . . splendour	(4.7)
2.15	stand firm	3.8
2.15	the traditions **which you have**	
	been taught by us	(4.1)
2.16	May our Lord Jesus **Christ**	
	himself and God our Father	
	(NB order)	3.11
2.17	encourage	(3.2)
3.1	And now, friends	4.1
	Pray for us	(5.25)
	word of the Lord	(1.8)
3.3	the Lord keeps faith	(5.24)
3.5	May the Lord **direct** your hearts	(3.11–13)
3.6	**These are our instructions**	
	to you, friends	(4.1)
	in the name of our Lord Jesus	
	Christ	(4.2)
3.6	idle	5.14
3.7	For you yourselves know	(5.2)
	follow **our** example	(1.8)
3.8	night and day in toil and	
	drudgery we worked for a	
	living rather than be a burden	
	to any of you	(2.9)
3.9	example	(1.6)

2 Thessalonians		1 Thessalonians
3.10	**during our stay** with you	(3.4)
	laid down this rule . . . work	(4.11)
3.12	**We urge such people** in the name of the Lord Jesus Christ	(4.2)
	to settle down to work and work **for a living**.	(4.11)
3.15	**admonish**	(5.14)
3.16	May the **Lord** of peace	(5.23)
3.18	The grace of our Lord Jesus Christ be with you **all**.	(5.28)

This gives us a comparative outline of the two letters which shows that just as 1 Thessalonians is shaped by the thanksgivings and prayer-wishes, the same is true of 2 Thessalonians.

Address and greeting	2 Thess. 1.1–21	1 Thess. 1.1
Thanksgiving and prayer	2 Thess. 1.3–12	1 Thess. 1.2–10
Thanksgiving	2 Thess. 2.13–14	1 Thess. 2.13
Prayer-wish	2 Thess. 2.16–17	1 Thess. 3.11–13
Request to pray for Paul	2 Thess. 3.1–2	1 Thess. 5.25
Faithful saying	2 Thess. 3.3	1 Thess. 5.24
Instructions	2 Thess. 3.4–15	1 Thess. 4.1–12
Prayer-wish	2 Thess. 3.16	1 Thess. 5.23
The grace	2 Thess. 3.18	1 Thess. 5.28

The comparative outline also indicates a number of key phrases, ideas and instructions which occur in both letters. A comparison of the two letters in the Greek texts shows up several key agreements in the choice of vocabulary which will be mentioned in the commentary.

It is probably unwise to make too much of any variations in the forms of address used in the two letters with reference to God and Christ (see Introduction, section 10). The balance between the work of God and that of Christ which we noted in 1 Thessalonians is maintained also in 2 Thessalonians. As far as the variation between 2 Thess. 1.1 and 1 Thess. 1.1 is concerned (see also 2 Thess. 1.11 'our God'; 2.16 'God our Father'), alongside that variation should be noted the agreement between 2 Thess. 2.16 and 1 Thess. 3.13, where both letters use 'our Father'. The form 'our God' is also found in both letters (see 2 Thess. 1.12 and 1 Thess. 3.9). Some scholars have argued that 'our God' and 'our Father' show that, whereas 1 Thessalonians was worded, in its initial section particularly, to engage the attention of Gentile converts, 2 Thessalonians is worded to engage the attention of Jewish Christians in the congregations. We shall see that there are pieces of evidence which suggest that a concern with Jewish Christians does affect the writing of 2 Thessalonians. But the choice of 'our God' and 'our Father' can hardly be made part of that evidence. While 1 Thessalonians may have used 'God' without the personal pronoun in 1 Thess. 1.2, 4, 8 and 9, to make a connection with Gentile converts to 'the living God', 2 Thessalonians can hardly be using the pronoun for the sake of Jewish Christian readers. 'Our' is inclusive, inclusive of both Gentile and Jewish Christians, and relational. In any case, if the addition 'our' shows anything, it is that 2 Thessalonians is written to bring different parts of the Christian community closer together, as indeed 1 Thess. 5.27 shows that 1 Thessalonians as a whole was.

The greeting
1.2

The fuller form of the initial greeting in 2 Thessalonians omits 'our' in the REB: *Grace to you and peace from God the Father and the Lord Jesus Christ* (1.2). It is likely that the REB text is correct; the addition of 'our' in some manuscripts of 2 Thess. 1.2 may well have been influenced by the uses of 'our Father' mentioned above. The presence in 1.2 of both grace and peace is interesting, because they appear together in Rom. 1.7; 1 Cor. 1.3; 2 Cor. 1.2 and elsewhere also, as a settled formula of greeting; and so too is the implied origin of grace and peace in both God the Father and Jesus Christ. The reference so early in the letter to 'peace' recalls its important role of 'peace' at the beginning of and especially in the later part of 1 Thess. 5.13–23; and the origin of 'grace' is both God and Christ according to the wider corpus of Pauline letters; as also is the origin of 'peace' (see Rom. 16.20: 'the God of peace', 'the grace of our Lord Jesus'). Such central qualities belong to both, as they are both the context which defines the Christian community's life (see the commentary on 1 Thess. 1.1 for an alternative translation of 2 Thess. 1.1). Instead of the REB's 'who belong to God our Father and the Lord Jesus Christ', we prefer 'in God our Father and the Lord Jesus Christ', since the latter is not only more literal as a translation but, like 2 Thess. 1.2, places the Thessalonian church within the total pattern of divine creation and redemption, as it provides a foundation for their election and call, and their share in the final glorification of Christ (2 Thess. 1.12).

The first thanksgiving and intercession
1.3–12

1.3 *Friends, we are always bound to thank God for you . . .* This opening thanksgiving in 2 Thessalonians illustrates how expansively thanksgiving to God can be, and ought to be, presented. There is much to thank God for. The expansion before God and before the hearers takes the form, as in 1 Thessalonians, of a long sentence in the Greek (2 Thess. 1.3–10), leading into a prayer of intercession (1.11–12) and is also expanded still further in 2.13–14 as another thanksgiving incorporating elements of both 2 Thess. 1.3 and 1 Thess. 1.4, 4.7–8 and 5.19.

We become aware of this expansiveness as we note the similarities and differences between 1 Thess. 1.3–10 and 2 Thess. 1.3–12. We noted in the commentary on 1 Thess. 1.3 that letters differ in one significant respect from a liturgical thanksgiving: it has an epistolary function, indicating some of the letter's concern and content; it is a communicative act, relating the concerns and content to the life of the particular community in and beyond the specific act of worship; it has a relational significance, introducing the authors and attempting to set the tone for the reading of the letter in its totality; it is a report of thanksgiving, made in relation to the background and history of the events which have been shared. So it depends as an opening section on the commitments, spirituality and values common to the writer and the hearers. All this helps us to be aware of the expansiveness of this thanksgiving. If, as we have suggested, 2 Thessalonians followed hard on the heels of 1 Thessalonians, there is bound to be an incremental element to this expansiveness. The authors build on what was said earlier and develop that in new directions.

As in the case of 1 Thessalonians the simplest way to see the section as a whole is to set out the REB translation, setting in bold

words and phrases which indicate links and underlining examples
where attention to the whole edifice is made easier.

Friends, we are always **obligated** to thank God **concerning** you, v.3
    as it is **proper** that we should,
    because your faith keeps on **growing abundantly**
    and the love you all have **each** for **the** other grows ever
        greater,
so that we **ourselves make our boast in** you among the churches
  of God   v.4
            concerning your **perseverance and** faith
            under all your persecutions and troubles
                you **are** enduring –   v.5
    clear evidence of the justice of God's judgement
        that you may be deemed worthy of the
            kingdom of God,
            for which indeed you are suffering –
if , that is, it is just **in God's sight to pay back affliction,**   v.6
    to those who afflict you, **affliction,**
        and to you who are afflicted, relief,   v.7
            along with us,
    at the **revelation of the** Lord Jesus from heaven with
      his mighty angels
                in blazing fire,
    in inflicting vengeance on those who refuse to
      acknowledge God   v.8
        and who do not obey the gospel of our
            Lord Jesus,
they it is who will suffer the penalty of eternal
  destruction   v.9
        from the presence of the Lord
        and the splendour of his might
        when he comes   v.10
            to be glorified in the sight of his **saints**
            and **to be a source of amazement because**
            of all believers,
            since our testimony to you was believed,
        on that day,
With **which** in mind we pray for you always   v.11
that our God may **make** you worthy of your calling
    that his power may bring to fulfilment

every **resolve to do good**
and every act inspired by faith,
<u>so that</u> the name of our Lord Jesus may be
    glorified in you,   v.12
        and you in him,
according to the grace of our God and the Lord Jesus Christ.

The outline suggests the main purpose of the thanksgiving. The Thessalonians have shown an abundance of faith and love (which is what 1 Thessalonians pleaded for), enabling Paul and his colleagues to boast of their faith and perseverance under persecution (it appears that the Thessalonian situation has worsened, 1.3–5a). The anxiety of the Thessalonians over their fitness for the kingdom of God has been brought to crisis point by the false alarm that the 'day of the Lord' has come; and Paul will argue that it is a false alarm since so much has yet to happen. In this thanksgiving, therefore, Paul describes their faith and perseverance as clear evidence of the justice of God's judgement – just, in two respects: first, in that they are deemed worthy of the kingdom for which they are suffering, 1.5bcd (so Paul, having thanked God for the progress in Thessalonica, confirms, against all their fears, the worthiness of the Thessalonians for the kingdom: 1.6); but just, secondly, perhaps in the afflicting of the afflicters, the relief of the afflicted at Christ's parousia, and in divine vengeance on those who do not know God and refuse to hear the gospel, but just most certainly in that it will be these who will suffer the ultimate penalties of separation from God, as against the share in glory of those who responded to the gospel, when the Lord is glorified, on that day. And it is with this in mind that Paul's intercessions are that God will bring to fulfilment all the works of goodness and faith so that a share in the Lord's glory may indeed be theirs through the grace of God and Christ. We described the growth of the thanksgiving as incremental. The outline illustrates well that complexity of growth.

1.3 *Friends, we are always bound to thank God for you, and it is right that we should . . .* Some regard 'bound to thank God' as a rather cool and unenthusiastic expression of praise (see 2.13, where it appears again). The following phrase 'it is right that we should' corrects that opinion. 'Right' means here what is appropriate to the context (see 1 Cor. 16.4), appropriate to the content and the pastoral circumstances of the thanksgiving. Far from being 'cool' the opening lifts the thanksgiving to the heights of the glory Paul is about to expound (the same is true of 2.13). It is pastorally right also since nothing less than delight and approval would be appropriate as a response to the progress which the Thessalonians have made, in the short time since 1 Thessalonians was received. Often these phrases are spoken of as liturgical, which may historically be correct, but gives a false impression of how they operate in a specific context.

1.3b . . . *because your faith keeps increasing, and the love you have for each other grows ever greater.* What is meant by a faith that increases? We have already seen that the Greek word '*pistis*', translated here 'faith' has a complex frame of reference. Here it 'keeps on increasing' (or, similarly durative, 'continues to produce abundant growth', see 2 Cor. 9.10 for the picture of organic growth: 'swell the harvest of your benevolence'; here, in 1.3b, the picture is further strengthened to indicate 'hyperabundance'). In what ways can faith show 'hyperabundance'? 1.3b has much that we found in 1 Thessalonians: affirmation of Jesus' death and resurrection (4.14); trust in Paul's testimony, a powerful defence (5.8); its need for its extension (3.10); and faithfulness (5.23). 2 Thessalonians adds an abundant growth in practical faithfulness (1.11); a tested faithfulness (2 Thess. 1.4b); a deepening commitment and trustworthiness (3.3); and the fulfilment of faith in sharing the Lord's ultimate glory (1.10). The growth of love among the Thessalonians also answers Paul's pleas in 1 Thessalonians. The love of the 'friends', for each other, has been more evident. We have no means of knowing Paul's evidence for this. One can only surmise that during the panic which we assume followed the false alarm the concern was shared and corporate. 1.11 prays for the fulfilment of every good resolve; and 2.10 links, by inference, love of truth to the goal of salvation. Like faithfulness, love has its source in the divine nature and activity (2.16), and as a practical human expression of that love faithfulness contributes to the present and future fulfilment of Paul's precepts.

1.4 *Indeed we boast about you among the churches of God, because your faith remains so steadfast under all the persecution and troubles you endure.* In 1 Thess. 2.19 we found Paul holding to his hope that at the parousia he could stand before the Lord with the Thessalonians as his joy and crown. We recognized there that, as in 1 Cor. 3.11–15, there was hope of reward at the parousia for work done in Christ.

Here in 2 Thess. 1.4 the boast is of what has been achieved in Christ's name and the boast is made to the surrounding churches (in Corinth and Achaia or more widely?). It is a boast which in the Greek text is made specifically by the missionaries, presumably as encouragement to the Thessalonians: 'so that we ourselves make the boast'. In 1 Thess. 1.8–9 the 'word of the Lord' rang out across Macedonia and Achaia, so that Paul need add nothing to what others had said. Now he can take up the theme himself. Boasting is a key word in Paul's ministry. He can only boast of the Lord (1 Cor. 1.27–29, quoting Jeremiah 9.24). As with several key examples of his vocabulary Paul can reduce their competitive edge, or at least attempt to do so – for example, he can boast that he has not made use of the rights to which he is entitled (see 1 Cor. 9.17; implied also in 1 Thess. 2.9). No doubt his occasions to boast could cause offence. They were sometimes part of a defence of himself such as orators used in forensic debates (see 2 Cor. 11.1—12.10; Long, pp. 186–90). That is hardly the case here. In part it is the addressees' perseverance and faith that are the subject of his boast; but 1 Thess. 2.10–14 links their self-offering to his own and that of his colleagues. There is room for pride in what they have achieved together in Christ's name. So Paul's boast here concerns the perseverance and faith of the Thessalonians during all that they are at present suffering. Their suffering involves being persecuted, the first time the term has been used in the Thessalonian correspondence (see Rom. 8.35; 2 Cor. 12.10; Mark 4.17). The precise meaning of 'persecution' is not clear; it would certainly not mean a deliberate attempt to eradicate Christianity from Thessalonica; it might more accurately be seen as intermittent periods of oppression (Malherbe, p. 388). Nevertheless, a worsening of the situation in Thessalonica is hinted at in 2.7,15–17; 3.3–35, which seems to have coincided with the false alarm regarding the 'day of the Lord'.

At this point in the thanksgiving we can compare what we have read with what we found in 1 Thessalonians. In 1 Thessalonians the triad of faith, love and hope characterized the Thessalonians' response to the missionaries' arrival, and the constant references to what they remembered built up a picture of the 'event in Thessalonica'. In 2 Thessalonians faith, love and perseverance form the triad (see the alternative triad in 1 Thess. 3.6) with a Christological basis for perseverance (see 2 Thess. 3.5; the context of the Thessalonians' progress is not the arrival of the missionaries but the worsened situation in the city).

1.5 *This points to the justice of God's judgement.* A glance at the outline of 2 Thess. 1 clarifies the position of this important passage within the argument of the whole thanksgiving. The REB's 'This points' is an addition to clarify the relationship of the phrase to what goes before. A close and relevant parallel is Phil. 1.28: You meet 'your opponents without so much as a tremor. This is a sure sign to them that destruction is in store for them and salvation for you.' Paul uses the word 'evidence' here, or possibly 'proof', of the justice of God's judgement. If it is 'proof' it has an active meaning, that which proves, rather than passive, that which is proved. What is evidence of the justice of God's judgement? Among the many answers to that question probably the most satisfactory is: what goes before – 'perseverance and faith under present persecution'. As for what follows there is a further problem regarding the relationship of 'God's judgement' to the following phrase. Normal New Testament grammatical rules would suggest that what follows is a result clause: 'with the result that you are made worthy' (Ellingworth, p. 138) or possibly a purpose clause. But in 1 Thess. 2.12 the same construction is used and without doubt in that context gives the content of what the father teaches. So we may translate 2 Thess. 1.5ab: 'clear evidence of the justice of God's judgement that you may be made [deemed] worthy of the kingdom of God'.

In what way is perseverance under suffering evidence of God's just judgement that the Thessalonians are worthy of the kingdom? The Old Testament provides evidence that suffering can be retributive (a chastising of the pious), prophetic of a reversal to come (Ps. 73) and evidence of election. So what is offered in 1.5 is present evidence, and, while it is prophetic of reversals to come, the suffering which the Thessalonians at present endure (1.5) is also evidence of the present work of God in the world. One of the Old Testament passages which leaves its mark on Paul's thinking in 2 Thessalonians is Isaiah 66. In Isa. 66.15 we find (in the Septuagint): 'Declare, our brethren, to those who hate and detest us, that the Lord's name is glorified and seen in their gladness.' Part of Paul's intention in this thanksgiving is to confirm for those who suffer that even the opposition they face is caught up in, and is evidence of, the divine purpose. The oppressors may be unwitting agents but they are evidence nevertheless. This is not to play down Paul's future expectation (see 1.12), but simply to add to it the present elements in his thanksgiving.

There is also another factor in the thanksgiving which needs to be noted. The reference just made to Isaiah 66 (and there are several literal quotations from Isaiah 66 in 2 Thessalonians) raises the question of to what extent Paul thought his letter would be intelligible to all the Thessalonians, to Jewish Christians and to previously pagan Christians and God-fearers. Certainly the pagans could not be expected to pick up the detailed Old Testament background which Paul assumes. The Jewish Christians, on the other hand, would be able to recognize in Paul's argument his wrestling with his own and with their own situation as converted Christians, especially concerning why among their opponents are Jews. The affirmation that, even in such opposition, the role of God could be understood was for Paul, as for them, an important consolation (see 2.11). The thanksgiving in 2 Thessalonians might well, in the light of these comments, be seen as more appropriately shaped for the Jewish Christians among the community in Thessalonica than for the previously pagan members. This would be intentional; perhaps Paul was aware that the false alarm might well have been taken up particularly by the Jewish Christians. 2 Thessalonians has their special needs in mind. But in no way were the Gentile Christian and the God-fearers excluded from the letter. The close parallels between 2 Thess. 1.1–12 and 1 Thess. 1.1–10 would reinforce the message originally given in 1 Thessalonians to those who experienced the Thessalonica event.

One particular point of translation in 1.5 still remains to be dealt with. In the clause which gives the content of God's judgement in 2 Thess. 1.5 does Paul mean that the Thessalonians 'will be proved worthy of the kingdom' (REB) or 'will be made worthy of the kingdom', or 'are made worthy of the kingdom (Ellingworth, p. 138), or 'deemed worthy of the kingdom'? In 1.11a the simple form of the same verb is found: 'we pray for you always, that God may count you worthy of your calling' (REB); parallel to this in 1.11b is 'that [God's] power may bring to fulfilment every good purpose'. Both parts of 1.11 may be future oriented, as in the REB: 'count you worthy of your calling'. That makes good sense in 1.11. On the other hand, the translation 'deemed worthy of the kingdom' has something to be said for it in both 1.5 and 1.11. The word 'deemed' is a present judgement which changes one's status, making the future fulfilment more realizable. In his letter to the Romans Paul made much of the idea of 'being deemed righteous', which implies both 'treating as' and 'giving the status of'. The parallel with 2 Thessalonians is interesting. The advantages of translating

2 Thess. 1.5 and 1.11 'may be deemed worthy' is that it adds a further emphasis in Paul's thankfulness for what God is doing in the present, without foreclosing on what God may do in the future.

We have reached the turning point in the 2 Thessalonians thanksgiving (see the outline of 1.3–12 above). From this point onwards we shall be reminded of the three practical areas with which the commentary began, the gravitational aspect of sin, the corruption involved in rapid change and the entanglement of human relationships. If the language of 1.6–9 seems foreign and repellent, it may be that this is because we resist facing the reality of human life; it may also be because translations of this passage have not always clarified the care with which Paul approached the problems of sin and its consequences. An illustration of this would be in 1.8 where some modern translations begin: 'He will punish those who do not obey God' (see NIV). This was not the way which Paul chose to address the human situation before God. So part of our task in commenting on 1.6–9 must be to try to do justice to the realities Paul confronts and to clarify that difficult area of his theological work.

1.6–9 This is a long conditional sentence: 'if . . .' (often called the protasis), 'then' . . . (often called the apodosis). There are two questions to be answered here: first, does 'if' imply 'if, and I believe this to be the case', or 'if, and it might be the case'? On the answer to that question major issues of Pauline theology depend. We shall deal with that presently. Second, where does the 'then' (the apodosis) start? Unfortunately in this 'sentence' Paul does not include the word 'then' or mark in some other obvious way the beginning of the apodosis. Dealing with the second question first: at the beginning of 1.9 there is a relative pronoun together with a verb; that could well be the demarcation we are looking for: 'they it is who'. That would mean that the 'if' clause (the protasis) stretches all the way from 1.6 to 1.8. Next, turning to the first question: does Paul mean 'if, and I believe this to be the case', or 'if, and it might be the case'? In the first kind of 'if' clause Paul is saying what he believes God does or will do; in the second he is reflecting on what God might do. Reading through 1.6–8 we come to the conclusion that in the first kind of protasis Paul believes God will do certain things which commit God to a detailed treatment of unbelievers (see 1.8), something which Paul never does anywhere else in his letters.

In the second he would be reflecting on what God might do (see v. 8).

The word 'if' at the beginning of 1.6 is a slightly unusual form of 'if' (the Greek *'eiper'*, rather than the simple *'ei'*). Some scholars argue that the special form in Paul's letters means 'if, and there is no doubt that' and some argue that it can mean in Paul's letters 'if, that is', registering hesitation and reflective consideration of what might be. The arguments about *'eiper'* are delicately poised, but there is just about enough evidence to make the second view possible. In Rom. 8.17 *'eiper'* introduces a condition which is not yet fulfilled and the consequence in the 'then' clause (the apodosis) is dependent on that fulfilment; the least we can conclude on Rom. 8.17 is that *'eiper'* there cannot mean 'if, and this is the case'. In 1 Cor. 15.15 *'eiper'* means 'if really, as they indeed say', although there *'eiper'* is accompanied by an additional Greek particle which affects how *'eiper'* functions. In 1 Cor. 8.5 it is certainly possible that the *'eiper'* protasis means 'for even granted that there are so-called gods, as indeed there are many "gods" and many "lords", yet for us there is but one God'. But does *'eiper'* actually mean that in 1 Cor. 8.5? Some scholars argue it could be 'concessive' there (that is, the condition is conceded as possibly although not necessarily true). The final answer on 1 Cor. 8.5 is affected by details concerning whether parts of the text are a quotation by Paul from Corinthian Christians and other parts of the text are his response. A recent Qumran discovery certainly gives strength to the view that 'gods' and 'lords' may represent real and recognized influences not at the divine level but at the level of angels, which would add a little weight to the 'for even granted that, and certainly there are' translation (Wold, pp. 158–9). But, given the likelihood of a conversation between Corinthian questioners and Paul (who has for argument's sake to assume their way of expressing their ideas), there may be just sufficient weight in the Greek of 1 Cor. 8.5 to set it alongside Rom. 8.17 and 1 Cor. 15.15. Given those two, and possibly three, examples it would be unwise to rule out *'eiper'* as capable of introducing an assumed or an as yet uncertain condition. How *'eiper'* should be translated may seem a curious detail to argue through to a conclusion; but we have in the above discussion, I believe, sufficient to support the view that in 2 Thess. 1.6 *'eiper'* does not necessarily state Paul's firm belief, and the significance of that is important: it allows us to interpret 1.6–9 alongside the rest of the Pauline letters without 2 Thess. 1.6–9 causing too much friction within that corpus. Yet another argument that has been used to suggest that 2 Thessalonians is not authentically Pauline is probably inconclusive.

During the discussion of 1 Thess. 1.10 we suggested that the REB translation 'retribution' was misleading, and that the Greek word '*orge*' was more accurately translated by 'wrath'; and that 'wrath' includes the disaster and chaos already at work, which will result in those who distance themselves from God being left to their own catastrophic devices. The question in 2 Thess. 1.6–9 is whether Paul, irrespective of what he does in 1 Thessalonians, commits himself to a retributive God in 2 Thessalonians.

Beginning with the protasis of the conditional sentence we translate 1.6: 'if, that is, it is *just* in God's sight to pay back affliction . . . To 'pay back affliction' (the literal translation) is a matter of an 'appropriate rendering in return'; the REB has '*balance the account*'. Paul uses the pattern of 'appropriate rendering back' not infrequently. As a pattern it has two sides to it: the one side is that human rebellion discovers the divine response of relinquishment (that is, of being left by God to one's own devices), with the consequence of chaos and corruption (relinquishment and corruption = 'wrath'); the opposite is that allegiance to God, which is where Paul places the emphasis, brings divine redemption and the consequence is eternal life. 2 Thess. 1.7 illustrates that pattern: *affliction to those who afflict you, relief to you who are afflicted* (a relief which is ours too, along with you). There is no question of retribution here, of God inflicting his 'wrath' as a penalty (Powys, pp. 326–50). It is the response of '<u>appropriate</u> rendering back'. Moreover, there is no question of Paul insisting that God inflicts a penalty on humanity; this section belongs to the protasis of the condition, which we have argued is not a statement of Paul's committed belief about God punishing unbelievers; it is the setting out of a possibility. 'If, that is,' Paul begins in 1.6, 'it is just in God's sight to pay back affliction', then what Paul is doing is setting out one way of seeing how God's justice may work: it may work not retributively, but by 'appropriate rendering back'. Failure in allegiance to God leads to abandonment by God, which leads to chaos and corruption, and, as we shall see, eventually to ruination and death. The pattern is now revisited at the level of the parousia (see 1 Thess. 1.10): *the revelation of the Lord Jesus from heaven with his mighty angels in blazing fire* (1.7cd). The final three words 'with blazing fire' reveal the source with which Paul is working in this section of the letter, Isa. 66 where we find 'See, the Lord will come like fire . . . to render back appropriately vengeance with wrath and a casting off utterly in flaming fire' (66.15, Septuagint). Why Paul is using this source and how he is using it, is nowhere made clear. Presumably he is using Isa. 66 (with its many facets of God's relationship with Israel) because some Thessalonians have been terrorized by the false alarm, and Paul initially must show them who needs to fear the 'day of the Lord', and who does not. How he is using Isa. 66 seems to be determined by reference to the 'appropiate giving back or rendering' pattern in relation to the parousia. Christ will come 'with flaming fire' could carry two different messages; the first message would be for those who have shown allegiance to God, who at the last may find Christ's presence a purifying fire (see 1 Cor. 3.15; that is, in terms of our discussion so far, they will need to depend on Christ at the parousia and on God making them worthy for his glorious kingdom). The second message is for those who rebel against God; in Paul's world view, God's casting off of various groups from his presence leads to their isolation from God, but that means, as the end product of their choice of chaos, eventual disintegration. This is not in any way to be confused with traditional ideas of hell. It is not God punishing immortal souls with undying flames; nowhere, for example, does Paul deal with the fate of the non-Christian dead. Paul is reflecting (see *'eiper'*) on what rebellion against God eventually could mean.

So in 1.6–7 we have been introduced to the pattern of 'appropriate giving back or rendering' in the context of the parousia. Moving on to 1.8 we find a verse which is deeply influenced by the language of Isa. 66. In Isa. 66.4 we find: 'I shall give appropriate rendering back to them for their sins, because I called them and they did not obey, I spoke to them and they did not listen', which is reflected in 2 Thess. 1.8: *who refuse to acknowledge God and who do not obey the gospel of our Lord Jesus*. We also find Isa. 66.15, referred to above: 'See , the Lord will come like fire . . . to render back appropriately vengeance with wrath and a casting off utterly in flaming fire', which is reflected by 'rendering *vengeance*' in 2 Thess. 1.8. The word which claims attention is translated 'vengeance'. Does Christ 'render vengeance'? There are four areas worth examining in relation to the word 'vengeance '(Greek *'ekdikesis'*). First, we have made the case for Paul in this conditional sentence exploring possibilities of divine justice, rather than stating how *'ekdikesis'* will happen. Second, both the 2 Thessalonian context and the Isaianic context use the verbs basic to 'appropriate rendering back'. Third, in

Isa. 66.15 there is the word 'with anger' accompanying '*ekdikesis*', and a very rare noun parallel to '*ekdikesis*' which means 'casting off utterly', a relational word concerning abandonment. Fourth, whereas in 1.6 the group indicated in the text are 'those who cause affliction', in 1.8 different groups are mentioned: 'those who do not acknowledge God' and 'those who do not obey the gospel' (the latter two groups are probably defined by activity rather than, for example, as Gentiles and Jews). The variations in the groups who are subject to the 'rendering back' pattern show how appropriateness works; it is certainly not precise retribution. In Rom. 2.7–10 the 'rendering back' pattern effects, first, for those who pursue honour and glory, immortality and eternal life; and, second, for those who are governed by selfish ambition, who 'refuse obedience to the truth and take evil for their guide', 'wrath, fury, tribulation and distress'. Those four considerations make it possible either for 2 Thess. 2.8 to be Paul's interpretation of the Isaiah prophecy in the Thessalonian context, or for '*ekdikesis*' to have a meaning here comparable with the classical Pauline 'appropriate rendering back' pattern as found in Rom. 2 and 12.19 (where '*ekdikesis*' and the verb 'rendering back appropriately' are side by side: 'Do not seek revenge but leave a place for "wrath" . . . For it is written: Vengeance is mine, says the Lord, I will render back appropriately, says the Lord').

We arrive now at the long-delayed apodosis in 2 Thess. 1.9. As in other '*eiper*' conditional sentences, the syntax is not straightforward. The apodosis begins with the relative pronoun (probably qualitative here), a pronoun which can designate a particular group. 'These are the ones who *will suffer the penalty of eternal destruction from the presence of the Lord and the splendour of his might.*' 'These are the ones' implies the distinction, assuming what has been suggested of how God's justice might work, between those of whom examples have been given in 1.6–8 and those like the Thessalonians in 1.3–4. The former experience 'wrath' and will know the final outcomes of 'wrath'; the latter experience 'life' and will know its outcome in eternal life shared in the company of Jesus Christ. Paul's point is clear: whatever may be said about the 'day of the Lord' and its timing, the Thessalonians have nothing to fear. Through God's grace and the redemptive work of Christ, the peace of God is their context of living, and eternal life in the kingdom of God will be their context at the last day (1.10). For the other groups 'wrath' is their experience and 'wrath, fury, tribulation and distress' await them.

There is, however, in 1.9 another term, in the Greek *'olethros'*, 'ruin' or 'destruction', which we met earlier in 1 Thess. 5.3. This is described as a just penalty, leaving them 'absent from the presence of God and his glory ('absent from' is one possible translation, and is preferred here because it continues the relational theme of presence with or absence from God; other possibilities are 'away from', 'after' or 'by'). The word *'olethros'* (1 Thess. 5.3) can mean 'ruin' or 'destruction'. So far we have concentrated on 'wrath' as God's relinquishing of those who reject him and his grace, that is, the relational aspect of 'wrath'. The translation 'destruction' would take this a stage further (as we saw in the case of 'with flaming fire' earlier, in 1.8). *'Olethros'* can imply that, since life is the gift of God, to deprive oneself voluntarily of God's life-giving presence means a kind of 'death' here and now; it also means that at the end 'wrath', if it does not include an ultimate realization of 'death', would lead almost inevitably in that direction. That understanding of *'olethros'* is not only relational, the relinquishing by God of the divine presence, but involves loss of 'eternal life' and in one sense or another it involves 'death', and finally therefore 'eternal death'. Paul calls this destruction 'the penalty they will pay'. Note that he does not say: the penalty God inflicts upon them. It has been their choice, and it is their fate.

Such a dramatic apodosis raises for the modern mind a host of questions. What is the reality of this 'choice'? Does 2 Thess. 1.5–9 reveal a free choice for life or death and a universally available choice? Does 2 Thess. 1.6–9 reveal an inevitable descent into chaos for some, or is salvation a universal possibility? When according to Paul is such an opportunity for repentance and salvation available, if it is not taken or available now? How could salvation be universal without the loss of human freedom to choose? This raft of problems, and these are only a few of them, cannot be answered in our context from Paul's texts; and certainly the difficulties we have encountered so far in translating Paul's texts accurately here are evidence enough that attempted answers to the above questions might not carry wide agreement. Nevertheless, what Paul is saying here has relevance in our contemporary world for the major questions which face us. He is presenting the universal problem of the chaos, distress and ruination which belonging to humanity can entail. He is claiming that God in Christ entered that reality in its total possibilities and dangers. He is convinced that the grace of God and of Christ provides through participation in Christ the fulfilment of God's purposes in our lives. He is himself wrestling with the meaning of 'election' and the effects and potentialities of 'wrath' (1 Thess. 2.14–16; Rom. 11.15–16). His pastoral intention is to confirm, for those who have made the choice to place their trust in this good news, that their commitment and perseverance will be honoured and they have no need to be anxious.

The parousia is a specific point of reference three times in the thanksgiving: in 1.7 where the 'appropriate rendering back' is ultimately linked to the 'revelation of the Lord Jesus from heaven with his mighty angels'; it occurs at the conclusion of the conditional sentence; and, third, it introduces the climax of the thanksgiving in 1.12. As we have seen, the conditional sentence 1.6–9 has the function of identifying groups which will suffer relinquishment at the parousia, so that the Thessalonians can be confident that at whatever time the parousia occurs they are safe from 'wrath'. But, as if to make clear that the confidence of the Thessalonians is his main concern, Paul describes the parousia at the end of the conditional sentence as follows: '*when he comes* to be glorified in *his* saints *and* to be the source of amazement because of *all believers, [and therefore* because of *you]*, because our testimony was believed as far as you are concerned, *on that day*' (1.10). The purpose of his coming is to be glorified. How the 'saints' fit into this glorious coming is indicated in the Greek of 1.10 and 1.12 by the same little preposition '*en*' which is capable of meaning 'among', 'in', 'by', and 'because of'. The verb 'to be glorified' is an unusual form in both 1.10 and 1.12, and the few Septuagint uses of the verb suggest that the little preposition could have any one of the four meanings. Because Paul is trying to strengthen the confidence of the Thessalonians it may well be best to regard the glorification of Christ at the parousia as seen from that point of view, that is 'to strengthen their confidence': he is glorified not only because he is who he is, the Lord, but also because of those who believe. As the Thessalonians will be Paul's crown, glory and joy at the parousia, so in a sense they represent the amazing work of Christ in his deliverance of them. The vocabulary is suited to thanksgiving and in liturgical language words like '*en*' can be deliberately ambiguous. They enrol a number of meanings to deepen the element of worship. So it would be appropriate to translate 1.10a 'to be glorified in his holy ones'; and, in order to make clear that the amazement at the Lord is in part amazement that he could draw together and deliver his saints, it might be best to translate 1.10b 'to be a source of amazement because of all believers'. But in that case the clause in 1.10c 'since our testimony was believed in your respect' adds the names of Paul, Silanus and Timothy to those who are a partial ancillary cause of the amazement at the Lord. That gives particular force to the curious position of *at that day*; it refers back as far as 1.9; it refers to 'when he comes' in 1.10a. But it also recognizes that 'on that day', the work of the missionaries in Thessalonica comes into its own as contributing to amazed wonder at the Lord's achievements. To enable that point to be expressed in the translation we suggest a bracket be added above to the REB translation: *[and therefore because of you]*. It is because of you, the Thessalonians, that the Lord is glorified in that day, but it is also because it is 'our testimony to you' which was believed.

The main thanksgiving spins along almost breathlessly with another relative clause: *with which in mind we pray for you always* (v. 11a). The thanksgiving section began with 'we are always obligated to give thanks for you' (1.3); it moved through gratitude for the abundant growth of faith and love during a time of persecution, and for the evidence there of God's justice in deeming the Thessalonians worthy of the kingdom; then into an affirmation that 'wrath' is not for the Thessalonians, rather they will share in the glorification of their Lord 'on that day'. An extraordinary span of thanksgiving. But that is not all. It is all incomplete without intercession. All this must be turned into fact; for that purpose (we not only give thanks but) 'we also intercede always for you'. The gratitude for God's choice of the Thessalonians, for their abundant faith and love, must flow by divine grace and help, into continued commitment. It needs commitment in the present; and in the future it needs divine fulfilment of their election (*that God may make you worthy of your calling*, 1.11b – probably the appropriate translation here). Commitment means the resolve to do good, and it means action based on faith: *that his power may bring to fulfilment every good resolve and every act inspired by faith* (1.11cd). So that is the content of Paul's prayer; its purpose, stated initially in the phrase 'with this in mind or for this purpose' (that is, for the glorification of and wonder at the Lord at his parousia) is then restated in the form: *so that the name of our Lord Jesus may be glorified in you and you in him* (1.12ab), another part quotation from Isa. 66. In Isa. 66.5 of the Septuagint those who hate Israel are to be informed that God's name will be glorified. So as a climax to the whole initial section of the letter Paul says that the Lord Jesus will be glorified in you, and then adds 'and you in him' (that is, 'you may be glorified in him'), a further stage beyond the recognition in 1.10 that the Lord would be glorified because of their place among the saints. The reported prayer (and the thanksgiving so far offered) is made *according to the grace of our God and of the Lord Jesus Christ* (see 1.2 and Introduction, section 10 for the unusual way in which Paul adds the definite article before 'God' and omits it before 'Lord'). Again the concluding words of the passage may be significant in relation to the climax of the prayer as well as to the whole of the section 1.3–12). It will be by divine grace, of God and of the Lord, that, despite all their uncertainties about themselves and anxieties about facing God at the parousia, the Thessalonians will share in the glory of the parousia (and presumably, therefore, of the kingdom: 1.5).

The 'day of the Lord'
2.1–12

A new section addresses the main problem which has caused the writing of 2 Thessalonians. *Now . . . we beg you, friends . . . about the coming of our Lord Jesus, when he is to gather us to himself.* The four parts of this opening show Paul imploring the Thessalonians (using the kinship reference, my friends). Paul designates the parousia as the subject of concern, which means in effect that in 2.2 the 'day of the Lord' and the parousia must be consonant with each other or overlapping to such an extent that for the purposes of Paul's letter they can be regarded as interchangeable; and he reminds them of what he has taught about the gathering up of dead and living to meet with the Lord, presumably through their attendance at the reading of 1 Thessalonians (1 Thess. 4.13–17). He implores them, *do not suddenly lose your heads, do not be* in a state of *alarm* (2.2a). The first begs them not to be shaken out of their wits; the second that they should not be terrified; together the two verbs reflect what happened when the false alarm was given. Some scholars give the verbs a quite different force, largely because they understand the Thessalonians to be overexcited at the thought of the parousia; they regard the emotion as excitement or a mixture of excitement and anxiety; they are 'wrought up' (see Song of Songs 5.4, Septuagint). The verb is in Greek '*throeisthai*'. This is a case where thorough examination of the meaning of a Greek word '*throeisthai*' using computer databases gives a clear meaning. The causative, passive forms mean 'to be terrified or disturbed', or, as in the REB, 'do not be alarmed' (see Mark 13.7 of the reaction to wars and rumours of wars, where the reaction there is paralleled in Luke 21.9 with a clear use of a 'terrify' verb). The history of the interpretation of Song of Songs 5.4 also probably points to 'consternation' ('wrought up' in that sense) rather than 'admiration' as the force of the verb (see Nicholl, pp. 128–30). In 2 Thess. 2.2 '*throeisthai*' is used in the present tense: to be in a state of alarm.

The first of the two verbs (as they stand in the text), translated in the REB 'lose your heads' is used here in a different tense from '*throeisthai*' and is accompanied by a preposition (as in 2 Kgs 21.8); the preposition suggests 'being violently shaken to remove from'; so in 2 Thess. 2.2 'to have been shaken out of one's understanding or critical judgement'. The importance of these studies is to confirm that (as in the REB) the reaction was fearful; more precisely the reaction of the Thessalonians to the false alarm was that they were shaken and left in a terrified state.

Paul now reveals his lack of precise information about how the false alarm was raised (see 3.11 for information that has reached Paul): 'do not be shaken out of your mind nor caused to be fearful' *by any prophetic utterance, any pronouncement, or any letter purporting to come from us* (2.2c). The damage has been done, but Paul wished to draw out from what had happened a warning to avoid any such disaster occurring again. The likelihood that there had been circulating a letter purporting to come from Paul is heightened by the ending of 2 Thessalonians: 'this greeting is in my own handwriting; all genuine letters of mine bear the same signature – Paul' (3.17). The likelihood is strengthened if, as in the REB, the phrase 'as if from us' refers to the third of the three possibilities: 'via a letter as if from us'. 'As if from us' could refer to all three means of communication, or indeed to the false message which follows; but the phrase reads most naturally if it is attached simply to 'a letter'.

That does not of course tell us the actual form of communication that brought the false report to the Thessalonians. It simply tells us that a letter may have been somewhere in the background. In 2 Thess. 2.17 Paul puts great emphasis on the means by which they have received teaching from him: 'hold fast to the traditions which you have learned from us by word or letter'. He has been able in his letters to ask them to recall what he taught them when present with them (see 1 Thess. 4.1); and as a written communication they had received 1 Thessalonians as a genuine response to Timothy's return.

These, Paul is warning, are the authoritative means of his communication. But that emphasis on his authoritative communications does not help us to identify what happened in the particular case of the false alarm. Any one of three, a prophetic word (see 1 Thess. 5.20), a proclamation of the word (1 Thess. 1.8), or a forged letter could have been the bearer to the Thessalonians of the false alarm: *alleging that the day of the Lord is already here* (2.2d).

As we have seen the most likely meaning of the 'day of the Lord' in this context is that it referred to the parousia (see 2.1). Some scholars take the view that the 'day of the Lord' might refer to a long period designated as the day of the Lord, including events spread over a period and involving severe tribulations and sufferings. But if this were the meaning of the 'day of the Lord' in 2 Thess. 2.2d then Paul's response that 'the day cannot come before the final rebellion' would make no sense; the day was understood, in the setting of the false alarm, to be a particular point within a sequence and not the sequence itself (2 Thess. 2.3). The difficulty is, as we have already pointed out, that Paul is implying an understanding of the 'day of Lord' which was specific, whereas in 1 Thess. 5.1–11 he was employing metaphorical and scriptural interpretations of the 'day of the Lord', interpretations which went back many centuries; and the purpose of his comments there was to indicate the style of life appropriate to believers.

It is for this reason that suspicion lingers around 1 Thess. 5.1–11 as the culprit behind the prophetic warning, or the proclaimed word or the forged letter, or if not the culprit at least that which made the false alarm believable. Timothy had confirmed the deep affection in which Paul was held in Thessalonica; and any word purporting to come from him via a primary or a secondary agency would have been listened to with serious attention. Hence Paul's current determination in 2 Thessalonians to establish his genuinely authoritative means of communication. Moreover, all the Thessalonians had been present when 1 Thessalonians was read, and the clear emphasis on 'the day' as the context of the Thessalonians' life and work could have lodged in the mind of a Jewish Christian in particular, affording an unmistakable resonance for the news that 'the day of the Lord is here'. Any claim to the authority of Paul behind that message would have given it immediate credence.

Why then should the coming of that message (however it came) have created 'a paralysing shock' and a 'continuing terror'? The best evidence we have as to how Paul understood their shock and terror is from 2 Thessalonians itself; and the two thanksgivings and the two prayer-wishes provide our safest guide. The thanksgiving 1.3–12 has three references to the parousia; the first appears in the long conditional sentence concerning appropriate rendering back, the second designates the groups to suffer 'wrath' and 'destruction', and contrasts these with the privilege of the Thessalonian believers, and the third sees the Thessalonians sharing the Lord's glory. The thanksgiving in 2.13–14 sets up a contrast between those who are deluded by the false alarm and Paul and his colleagues; it reiterates that the sharing of the Lord's glory by the Thessalonians is the purpose behind God's election of them, the sanctifying work of the Spirit and their belief in the truth. These two thanksgivings are both designed to distinguish the Thessalonians who will be glorified and those who for various reasons are the ones who will come under 'wrath'. The two prayer-wishes deal, first (2.16–17), with their strengthening in deed and word on the basis of the encouragement and hope offered by the divine love and grace, and, second (3.16), with the hope that the God of peace will give them peace at all times and in all ways. In the light of those key passages in 2 Thessalonians, Paul's undertanding of the shaken and fearful state would seem to be that they do not appreciate the difference between themselves as the elect who believe the truth, are being sanctified in word and deed, and have the promise of glory with the Lord, and those who through rebellion and through the delusion concerning the parousia are 'doomed to destruction'. The most likely way then in which Paul saw the Thessalonians as shaken and in fear because of the false alarm is that he saw them as fearful that the 'day of the Lord' would mean judgement for them and that their improvement and sanctification in deed and word were still far short of what would be required 'on that day'. The news that the 'day of the Lord' had arrived was therefore a moment of shock and was greeted with unabating horror. Paul would recall that the deaths in the Christian community had caused horror for the same reason, and Paul had tried to assure them of the ways in which divine grace could see them all, including their deceased friends, in the final company of Christ. The Thessalonians may well have taken in what Paul had taught them, but the existential moment of facing the day of the Lord awoke all their basic fears and anxieties. They were not ready, and they knew they were not ready.

It is worth comparing the way in which such a solution to the question 'Why were they shaken and afraid?' fits with the context of both 1 and 2 Thessalonians, and the lack of fit which other solutions betray. For example, it has been suggested that what made them shaken and afraid was the absence of any signs of the parousia, leading the Thessalonians to think that they had been bypassed. Like the fate they feared for their deceased colleagues they felt that they had missed out on the blessings of the kingdom. Such a solution picks up some aspects of the glory which Paul promises them, but fails to meet the clear contrast in character and fate which Paul establishes, in both the thanksgivings, between the Thessalonians who believe and the fate of those who are deluded and have failed to believe.

The response to the false alarm in 2 Thess. 2.3 begins with a warning against delusion, which will be examined later in the chapter: *Let no one deceive you in any way.* Deception and delusion should have no part in the life of those who have opened their minds to the love of truth (2.10). The argument which follows takes up various stages of 'wrath'. 'Wrath' has already been at work (1 Thess. 2.14–16), but 'wrath' is incremental as Scripture makes clear, and the 'wrath' of the day of the Lord (1 Thess. 1.10) is a climax to the many expressions of chaos, disaster, rebellion and death. *That day cannot come before* the apostasy, and when the man of rebellion (or lawlessness) *will be revealed . . .* (2.3c). This verse summarizes two ways in which the Thessalonians can be sure that the 'day of the Lord' has not yet come: there must be apostasy, a wholesale rebellion against God; and there must be a focus of rebellion in the revealing of a human being who personalizes rebellion. Why these must happen, and how the Thessalonians should know that these things must happen, will be part of Paul's argument in 2.3–12.

The passage in Isa. 66.1–5 to which we have already referred concerns the disobedient who will receive the 'appropriate rendering back' of their disobedience; it also includes 'the rebel' (the lawless man) who in face of the Lord of creation chooses all manner of what is abhorrent to the Lord. The Lord who has respect for the humble, the quiet ones, the ones who fear God's words, will repay 'the rebel'. 'Rebellious children' appear also in Isa. 57.3–5 (Septuagint), a lawless breed associated with adultery and idolatry, 'children doomed to destruction' (see 2 Thess. 2.3d). The rebel is *'the son doomed to destruction'* (see Ps. 88.23, Septuagint). His revelation, his public appearance, must, if Scripture is to be fulfilled, happen before the 'day of the Lord', as he must meet his doom at the dawning of the 'day of the Lord' (2.8). The 'day of the Lord' must still be future.

At this point in Paul's response to the false alarm he begins to use the tradition from the book of Daniel, which provides a line of clues to the cryptic comments in 2.4–8. The 'rebel' (the man of lawlessness), 'the son doomed to destruction', becomes the antagonist, the antagonist against God and against his people. *He is the adversary who raises himself up against every so-called god or object of worship, and even enthrones himself in God's temple, claiming to be* [or proclaiming publicly, or designating himself to be] *God* (2.4). This is the one who will be revealed. In Dan. 11.36 a king 'exalts and magnifies himself'; in the setting of Daniel he is Antiochus Epiphanes, the opponent of Israel's God and his people, the Jews; in 2 Thessalonians he becomes the future opponent of God and his people, a people which includes the Thessalonians; he will magnify himself above every god and against the God of gods he will utter monstrous blasphemies; things will go well with him until the 'wrath' 'is spent'. The characteristic of this figure is self-exaltation, exaltation over all the so-called gods (see 1 Cor. 8.5 and the comments there on 2 Thess. 1.5 regarding heavenly influences, powers and angels), and over objects of worship (the word is used in Wisd. 14.20 of a human being raised by superstitious veneration to a figure of worship). His main recognizable characteristic is his supreme blasphemy; he seats himself in the Jerusalem Temple (see Isa. 66.1), claiming to be God. The traditions about past historical figures, such as the Emperor Caligula who had similar pretensions, fastened on to Dan. 11.36–37, but there was no one who quite realized in the Temple in Jerusalem that gravest of blasphemies; the supreme 'rebel' was still in Paul's day, a future monstrosity (what probably became known in the Synoptic Gospel tradition as the 'abomination of desolation': Dan. 12.11); and what he would eventually do would be a public spectacle which all would recognize. The 'day of the Lord' could not happen until that publicly known event.

These scriptural passages and traditions had been used during the missionaries' work in Thessalonica; the Greek text suggests that they had been frequently used. The stages of 'wrath' formed an element in Paul's message; they are now seen as building up a terrifying picture of evil against which God's deliverance in Christ could be experienced as deliverance and redemption: *Do you not remember that I told you this* (often) *while I was still with you* (2.7). The scriptural background for this sequence could hardly have been known except among the Jewish Christians and the God-fearers; even the mythical background which pagans would have been able to recognize, and which will become evident in 2.6–8, could only have been used by Paul in a Jewish Christian adaptation. How Paul could have expected the Gentile Christian to take in these details (see 1 Thess. 1.9–10) is by no means clear. However, of immediate relevance to both Jewish and Gentile Christians were the persecutions and tribulations they were enduring; these would have given to Paul's strange language about wrath, evil, rebellion and apostasy immediate reality and a warning that there was more still to come.

2 Thess. 2.6 is strange language indeed, and has puzzled many generations of readers. Yet Paul emphasizes that this was already part of their Christian store of knowledge, if only they had taken it in: *You know, too, about the restraining power which ensures that he* [the 'rebel'] *will be revealed only at his appointed time* (presumably at the point God had allocated). They know about the 'rebel'; they know also what has temporarily had the responsibility of holding the 'rebel' back from appearing publicly and publicly committing the ultimate blasphemies. It is the 'restraining power'. Until very recently this cryptic reference had seemed unintelligible. But various pieces of evidence now point to the restraining power being another of the personae in Daniel chapters 11—12: the archangel Michael (Nicholl, pp. 225–49). The REB text in Daniel reads: 'At that time there will appear Michael the great captain, who stands guarding your fellow-countrymen, and there will be a period of anguish such as has never been known ever since they became a nation till that moment' (Dan. 12.1abc; the purpose of the period of anguish being, presumably, to purify and hallow the people: Dan. 12.10). Michael is the guardian of God's people; a restraining hand on wickedness and persecution, for Christians, according to 2 Thess. 2.6, as he was for the Jews according to the book of Daniel. But of course the REB text is only one translation of one version of the book of Daniel. Recently, a version of Dan. 12.1 has come to light which has one major difference; instead of Michael 'appearing' (as in the text just quoted), it has Michael 'withdrawing', 'stepping aside'. Michael is their guardian; but once he steps aside 'there will be a period of anguish such as has never been known ever since they became a nation till that moment'. The one who ensures that the 'rebel' will be revealed only at God's appointed time steps aside, and 'all hell' can break loose: the 'rebel' will be able to commit all the blasphemous acts of which he is capable.

How do the Thessalonians know this? They know it beause they have been taught by Paul; they know it also because *already the secret forces of wickedness* (of rebellion), known only at the moment as a mystery (the secrets of which human intelligence cannot pierce) *are at work*, at work *only until the* one who hitherto acts as restrainer *is removed from the scene* (2 Thess. 2.7). Once again, if only for a moment, Paul switches from his strange and cryptic language to the experience of the Thessalonians. They have in their short time as Christians witnessed many forms of rebellion and 'wrath', and have been puzzled and troubled by them. Paul now explains why, as yet, it has been so puzzling and mysterious. It is because the 'restrainer' has so far ensured that it remains limited and mysterious. Presumably Michael is in the heavenly places using his powers as an archangel to prevent the release on earth of the 'rebel' (Michael presumably resembles the powers in the ancient mythical creation stories of how chaos was held in check). Once he steps aside, instead of the forces of rebellion being mysterious, they become personalized, public, horrific and far more danger- ous. But this is all a matter of the divine purpose. As far as the Thessalonians are concerned all is in God's hands. So *then he* [the 'rebel'] *will be revealed, the wicked* [rebellious] *one . . .* (2.8a). We have reached the point with which Paul began in 2.3; this is the moment which must happen before the 'day of the Lord' can come. The 'rebel' must appear first, because he is the one *whom the Lord Jesus will destroy with the breath of his mouth and annihilate* at the epiphany [the dawning?] of his Parousia (2.8bc).

There is still, however, much to say about the 'rebel', particularly about the deception and delusion which accompanies his work. *The* parousia *of the wicked one* (he has become a sort of anti-Christ who inaugurates humanity's apostasy) is enabled *by the work of Satan*; he comes in falsehood's full power, with *signs and miracles*, and in full *deception* of that wickedness as far as concerns those who are *doomed to destruction* (2.9–10a). What had been known as a power, mysteri- ous and limited, albeit real and experienced, will be recognized at this stage in its full potential to deceive and delude those who *do not open their minds to love of the truth and so find salvation* (2.10b). 'The love of the truth' is an unexpected phrase: those who do not give attention and commitment (that would serve as a summary in this context of the word 'love') to the gospel (that is part of the meaning of 'truth' here) make themselves (and they carry responsibility for this) vulnerable at this stage of greatest danger, since 'the Satan' has such power to delude (suggesting by contrast another aspect of 'truth'). Of all the full powers of the Satan which Paul might have enumerated he selects the one most crucial at the moment of the writing of 2 Thessalonians both for the readers and as a part of his total argument: delusion, since that can lead to loss of salvation. Those who have refused to commit themselves to the truth of the gospel find that God has delivered to them the power to capitulate to error, and so become bound to falsehood. The REB prefers the paraphrase 'a compelling delusion' (the phrase means literally 'a working power of error'): *That is why God puts them under a compelling delusion which makes them believe what is false.* But the REB version, 'puts them under a compelling delusion' would largely cancel out the responsibility given by Paul in the previous verse. God does indeed 'harden the hearts of unbelievers' according to the New Testament (Rom. 11.25), as via 'wrath' humanity has the freedom to choose chaos. But the REB translation would, in the context of the Satan's full expression of power before the annihilation of the the 'rebel', extend that hardening to an inexorable and final hardening of the heart rather than hardening of the heart to bring the unbelievers to repentance. It could of course be that Paul intends 2.10 to refer only to the present, and the verb is in the present tense. But 'them' in 2.11 refers to the 'doomed' ones, afflicted by the Satan's full power in v. 10. A totally present interpretation of 2.11 is improbable. 'That is why God delivers to them a working power of error' would fit both future and present contexts. This would also concur with 2.12, which uses the phrase 'have set their resolve on wickedness': *so that all who have not believed the truth but made sinfulness their choice may be brought to judgement* (2.12).

The second thanksgiving
2.13–14

The second thanksgiving (2.13–14) sets up a contrast with the delusion and doom of those who do not 'love the truth'. The contrast is deliberately marked in the Greek text but not in the REB. The initial contrast is between those who do not believe in the truth and the missionaries who find themselves still obligated to give thanks to God for the Thessalonians. The second contrast is between those who are doomed to destruction and those who are 'the beloved by the Lord' 'chosen to find salvation'. There may, however, be an even more fundamental contrast intended. The translations of 2.13 are as evenly divided as is the manuscript evidence: at 2.13 the REB, KJV, NASB, and JB all read: 'from the beginning God chose you'; the NIV, GNB, Moffatt and Knox all read: 'God chose you as firstfuits'. So, for example, the REB reads: *We are always bound to thank God for you, my friends beloved by the Lord. From the beginning of time God chose you to find salvation in the Spirit who consecrates you and in the truth you believe.* The main argument against 'from the beginning' is that there are two other places where scribes probably misread the text; the same sequence of letters in the text originally meant 'firstfruits', yet the scribes saw 'from the beginning'. If 'firstfruits' is the better translation then it has a double reference, 'God's firstfruits' are an encouragement to the missionaries (. . . 'But we are obligated to give thanks . . .) in the middle of all the grief and ruin reflected in 2 Thess. 1.12 and 2.10–12. God's firstfruits encourage them to believe that others will respond. The second part of the double reference is to 'the firstfruits in Thessalonica'; this offers encouragement to the Thessalonians that there will be others of their townsfolk who will follow their example. The believing community may be small, and the Satan in full power a daunting prospect, but from the divine perspective there will be many more to join them in 'possessing the splendour of our Lord Jesus' (2.14c); and there will be time for this harvest. As against the deluding devices of the Satan, which might threaten their confidence, the Thessalonians have the election of God to salvation to give them heart (see 1 Thess. 5.9), the work of the Holy Spirit consecrating their lives, and God's power strengthening them to believe in the truth. The contrasts between believers and non-believers are being developed throughout the verse.

It was for this [also] *that he called you through the gospel we brought, so that you might come to possess the splendour of our Lord Jesus Christ* (2.14). 'For this' refers back to 'salvation' in the previous sentence and to the continuing work of the Spirit and belief in the truth of the gospel. That was the purpose of God's call and the call came specifically through the proclamation of the missionaries. Some manuscripts read the word 'also' after the opening words 'For this'. It is a tempting addition and it changes the function of 2.14. As it stands in the REB, 2.14 reminds the hearers of the part which the missionaries played. If we add 'also' to our text, 'for this also' still picks up the previous verse; but it also points forward to the complete possession of a share in the Lord's glory. The function

111

of 2.14 is then to remind the Thessalonians of the promise which resounds through 1 Thessalonians (see especially in 5.9) and which appears also in 2 Thess. 1.3–12, the promise of full attainment of salvation. The Thessalonians have been well aware of the process by which they have been assisted in the Christian life through the many means of divine grace; their anxiety was whether they would in the end be worthy, whether they would attain full salvation. If we read 'For this also', 2.14 again underlines the fulfilment of that promise.

Paul has reached an important conclusion in his argument: he begins the next verse: 'So then'. So then *stand firm . . . my friends, and hold fast to the traditions which you have learned from us by word or letter* (2.15). His conclusion is that, for a safe and secure footing they should rely only on what he has taught them and on what has reached them by properly attested means, whether orally or written. Failure to do that has cost them unnecessary anxiety and terror.

The first prayer-wish
2.16–17

2.16–17 transforms the conclusion in 2.13–15 into a prayer-wish. The invocation is in some respects unusual. The order, first the Lord Jesus Christ, and, second, God our Father, is found in Gal. 1.1 where, as in 2 Thess. 2.16, 'God the Father' is expanded using participial descriptions (which appear in the REB translations as relative clauses): *And may our Lord Jesus Christ himself and God our Father, who has shown us such love, and in his grace has given us such unfailing encouragement and so sure a hope, still encourage and strengthen you* [see 1 Thess. 3.13] *in every good deed and word* (2.16–17). Some regard the participles (or, in the REB, relative clauses) as descriptive of both Christ and God; but it is more likely that Christ is named first because the subject of the section has been the 'day of the Lord', and the participles (or clauses) belong with 'God our Father', so that all that Christ has done and will do is seen in the context of divine saving care for all the followers of Christ (Wanamaker, p. 270). God's love will be given particular emphasis in the next prayer-wish in 2 Thess. 3.5; his grace is seen to be a major and unfailing encouragement, and we shall comment further on this later; the safeguarding of the future for the Thessalonians is marked by the sureness of the hope which God has given. All these gifts are already part of the Thessalonians' experience. Significantly the item which is mentioned last, 'every good word and deed', is the crucial means by which the Thessalonians can prepare themselves, in so far as this is possible, for the parousia and coming face to face with God.

Many might regard 2 Thess. 2.1–14 as a curious passage with little relevance for a world like our own, which is so differently structured from Paul's world. It has, however, an invaluable comment to make of relevance to our generation in particular. It is concerned with a chaos, in which wickedness moves from a mysterious and mystifying reality to an extraordinarily powerful embodiment of evil. Yet the grace of God is always greater than the worst scenarios, and the divine summons of a people called to witness to that grace seems, despite their apparent inadequacy, to remain a sustainable project while many others across the years have failed. That at least is a vision Paul can share with us.

Intercession and faithfulness
3.1–4

The chapter opens with the same introduction we found in 1 Thess. 4.1; there we questioned whether it could be allocated a precise function or meaning. The problem is slightly easier here in that, immediately after 3.1–4, a second prayer-wish is inserted in 3.5. So 3.1 is likely to be a general section marker rather than a specific indicator such as 'finally': *And now, friends, pray for us, that the word of the Lord may have everywhere the swift and glorious success it has had among you* (3.1). By contrast with the brevity of the similar request in 1 Thess. 5.25 this is an extended request for the Thessalonians to support the missionaries with intercessory prayer. The content of the prayer-request is that 'the swift and glorious success' the word of the Lord 'has had among you' may be repeated wherever the missionaries work. 'The word of the Lord' recalls 1 Thess. 1.8, where the word of the Lord (both proclamation and response) rang out across Macedonia and Achaia and even more widely, carrying the story of 'the Thessalonica event'. The metaphor in 2 Thess. 3.1 is different. In 1 Thess. 1.7 the picture was of a resonating sound carrying across the landscape; in 3.1 it is a picture found elsewhere in Paul, of the athletic games, concentrating as in 1 Cor. 9.24–27 on speed and success. (A parallel in Ps. 147.4[15] has the Lord's word running swiftly but not explicitly with success; Zech 5.1–14 has God sending out a flying scroll with immediate success but with devastating effect.) The request is that the work of the missionaries may resemble that of the Thessalonians (see 2 Thess. 2.13, where God's firstfruits resulting from the missionaries' work promise a further harvest, just as the firstfruits of Thessalonica promise further success among the local population). Paul's use of the comparison between the two missions may be intended as an encouragement to the Thessalonians, but it is rather more than that. The request is for support within an enterprise to which both the authors of the letter and those who receive it are mutually committed; hence mutual support can be relied upon. How different the situation which faces Paul and his colleagues in Corinth! The second part of the prayer-request reveals a very different context: *and that we may be rescued from wrong-headed and wicked people; for not all have faith*. There are two problems of translation in 2 Thess. 3.2. 'Wrong-headed' is an unexpected term in the REB and in the Greek. The word translated there, *'atopos'*, has a wide range of possible meanings (see Frame, p. 293) and might designate troublemakers or the immoral in Corinth (see Acts 18.6; and Chrysostom, *Homilies on Matthew* 43.2), or troublemaking Jews as in Rom. 15.30–31. It could also mean 'unreasonable' people on whom Paul cannot rely. The second problem is the phrase translated 'for not all have faith'; it might well mean 'for faithfulness is not found in everyone'. Clearly there is a contrast intended between 3.2b and 3.3. In 2 Thess. 3.2 there are unreliable Corinthians; in 2 Thess. 3.3 Paul affirms God's faithfulness; *he will strengthen you and guard you from the evil one* (see the prayer-wish in 2.17). The previous section of the letter has given space to the powers which evil (either impersonal or personalized) can exert. For the Thessalonians to be faithful to the vocation God has given them, God must give them the protection they need; and the missionaries have put their trust in the Lord with respect to the Thessalonians that they will both now and hereafter follow the precepts given them: *we have confidence about you that you are doing and will continue to do what we tell you* (3.4). The unit hinges on faithfulness, God's faithfulness, and what that means for the security, the relationships and the style of life of those who believe in such a God (White, pp. 25–43, 106–48). That may also explain Paul's sense of frustration at those who are unreliable and wicked, even perhaps among the people he is working with in Corinth.

The second prayer-wish
3.5

The prayer-wish places God's faithfulness in its most impressive setting, that divine love which never fails or disappoints, which meets the different circumstances of human need effectively and surely (see 2.8–17): The use of the name 'Lord' is ambiguous; it probably refers to God, as is the case almost certainly in the parallel prayer-wish in 3.16. The two passages run: *May the Lord direct your hearts towards God's love . . .* (3.5a); 'May the Lord of peace himself give you peace' (3.16). The prayer-wish that God will direct their hearts states a second goal, that form of faithfulness which Christ showed and which has been the constant theme of the Thessalonian correspondence: Christ's steadfastness, as the model and the means by which the Thessalonians may follow him. ('Model' corresponds to 'imitation' as 'means' corresponds to 'participation'; see Introduction, section 10.) The unit, therefore, brings together divine faithfulness and the faithfulness expected of the Thessalonians in the changing cirumstances of their life, as they both do and will do what Paul's precepts have taught them.

Disciplining the idle
3.6–15

Paul now reverts to a subject he has dealt with at least twice before: working for a living. But something has changed. Originally he had recommended his own choice of manual labour or his own choice to demean himself by manual labour; he sees this choice as preventing him from being a financial burden on the Thessalonians (1 Thess. 2.9). On the second occasion he placed manual labour in the context of 'love for the "friends"' and a means of keeping a social profile which in the permeability of the community boundaries would bring general respect and some level of economic independence. But this third reference has a sharper edge to it; instead of attending to his advice some are simply being idle, even perhaps choosing to be idle, and the community in Thessalonica has to find a pastoral way of correcting this development. We might ask why this should be such an important issue and why Paul should make a point of seeking to correct it. His policy while living in Corinth was to work wth his hands, and later, in 1 Corinthians, he refers back to this policy and places his choice within his wider attempt to structure and transform the Corinthian Christian community. He is consciously identifying himself with the economically weak (Horrell, 1996, pp. 202–3). In the Thessalonian correspondence we can see the beginnings of this policy; he saw the 'Thessalonica event' as a recognition of how important identifying with the poor could be.

Paul also stresses the importance of this issue by the term which he uses for the idle; he calls their behaviour 'disorderly'. If the voluntary associations were well known or even a part of the Thessalonian Christian community life, 'disorderly' would include those who did not 'pull their weight' and they would be dealt with by the disciplinary code of the association. The REB uses the translation 'falling into idle habits', but it has to be remembered that this is regarded as disorderly conduct – as unacceptable and deliberately disobedient behaviour.

But how to correct those who refused manual labour and chose to be disorderly? It has to be through a means which corrects without discouraging, which admonishes without driving away, and which draws attention to the need for manual labour without causing a split in the community's life. Paul's counsel is: *hold aloof from every Christian who* practises *idle habits, and disregards the tradition you received from us* (3.8b). He calls this *our instructions to you, friends, in the name of our Lord Jesus* (3.8a). What has to be done is 'within the love of the "friends"', within the establishing of the family relationships within the community, and not on the authority of Paul but 'in the name of the Lord'. Paul calls up the memory of what he had said on the subject before; his previous advice had been to accept his working pattern as a model for imitation. *You yourselves know how you ought to follow our example; you never saw us idling* (3.8). This would be later how he described his pattern of life in Corinth. At the time of the Thessalonian correspondence he was living out this standard in his current base; and from their own memory of the 'Thessalonica event' the Thessalonians could confirm that Paul and his colleagues had behaved as orderly artisans should.

There was another factor in Paul's choice of manual labour: *we did not accept free hospitality from anyone; night and day in toil and drudgery we worked for a living, rather than be a burden to any of you – not because we do not have the right to maintenance, but to set an example for you to follow* (3.8–9). Paul's refusal of hospitality has at least four facets: the intention to be independent of the Thessalonians financially (although not from the Philippians!); the desire not to be a burden to them; the refusal of patronage of any kind; and the recognition of rights as a missionary apostle which he could deliberately choose to deny himself. Behind these four facets lies the likelihood that there were people among the Thessalonian community who could have provided at least some finance. To those Paul denies the privilege of being charitable; as in the Corinthian situation Paul allows little room for what has been called 'love patriarchalism'. His policy for the development of the Christian community is marked out by his choice of manual labour and his refusal to accept inevitable social differences as determinative of the structure of Christian community life.

This policy has a direct relevance to the disciplining of 'idlers'. Those who choose not to work are making themselves dependent on the richer members, and that is subversive of the kind of community Paul seeks. They probably also have been taking advantage of 'a common table', the sharing at meal times of available food. If there were special community meals (the Lord's Supper for example) then that would be an opportunity for eating what others provided. The cutting edge of Paul's disciplinary instruction was: *Already during our time with you we* used to lay *down this rule: anyone who will not work shall not eat* (3.10). This Pauline instruction carried his own personal agenda. It was a common enough guideline in ancient society, and an early Christian document, the Didache, has a section detailing how this problem of idleness should be dealt with. But Paul's agenda is the correction of disorder through discipline, a discipline which, apparently on the basis of 3.10, he intends should exclude an idler from community meals, or meals which were provided on a charitable basis. This gives teeth to the general instruction in 3.6 'to hold aloof from every Christian who behaves in a disorderly way'. This cannot have meant exclusion from the Christian community as such. That would have been too draconian, involving all the problems we listed earlier. Nevertheless, there was an element of 'shaming' such people so as to bring them back to their right mind: *We mention this because we hear that some of you are idling their time away, minding everybody's business but their own. We instruct and urge such people in the name of the Lord Jesus Christ to settle down to work and* eat their own food (3.11–12). Moffatt's paraphrase of 3.11 catches the neatness of Paul's comment: they are being 'busybodies instead of busy' – the well-known problem in the ancient world (to say nothing of today) of meddling in other people's affairs. But behind the meddlesome pattern lies a disobedience which Paul deplores; he 'urges and instructs' them, repeating as in 3.6 that this is 'in the name of the Lord Jesus Christ', to abide by the instructions he had already given them at the public reading of 1 Thessalonians. They had not heeded his words; so discipline must follow. The whole community now must take on board what Paul has said originally; he now lays firmly on the whole community the responsibility of shaming the idlers and returning them to orderly behaviour: *My friends, you must never tire of doing right.* (That sentence could be addressed both individually to the idlers, and corporately to the whole community. He continues to address everyone directly.) *If anyone disobeys the instructions given* via *my letter* [Does Paul mean the letter he originally wrote or the letter he is now writing? Presumably 'disobeys' refers to his current attempt to sort the disorder out], *single him out, and have nothing to do with him until he is ashamed of himself. I do not mean treat him as an enemy, but admonish him as one of the family* (3.13–15). The instruction 'single him out and have nothing to do with him' may not be quite what Paul intended. The Greek text probably originally intended 'single him out' to be qualified by 'so as not to associate with him until he is ashamed of himself'. There is no lasting opprobrium or disgrace; nor is there to be animosity raised in the admonishing; the admonishing (which Paul had actually asked for in 1 Thess. 5.14, with perhaps a hint there that leaders might have a role in this, see 1 Thess. 5.12) now becomes and is to remain a family responsibility.

The final prayer-wish
3.16

The community needs (as it did in 1 Thess. 5.23) the prayer-wish for peace, peace as the resolution of the disorder, in the process of community discipline, and thereafter in the restoration of harmonious relations. There is also the restoration of peace of mind and heart to pray for after the disastrous 'false alarm', a restoration to which Paul hopes to have made a contribution. Then there are the incessant disturbances by those who wish them no good: *May the Lord of peace himself give you peace at all times and in all ways. The Lord be with you all* (3.16; turning the affirmation of 1 Thess. 1.1 and 2 Thess. 1.1 into a form of blessing).

The signature
3.17

Paul can use his own handwriting to make a polemical point at the end of a letter (see Gal. 6.11–16); and in a sense that is what he is doing here, reminding the community of their gullibility in accepting as authentic the false alarm and perhaps their readiness to think that a letter circulating in his name had actually been written by him. Of course, if the problem had been a copy of 1 Thessalonians, misunderstood by those to whom it was not originally written, then Paul's addendum here would not have provided the necessary safeguard. But Paul was not in a position to know if that was the problem. All he intends is that from now on they should look for his signature before giving way to panic: *This greeting is in my own handwriting; all genuine letters of mine bear this same signature – Paul.*

The grace
3.18

The end of the letter is interesting for several reasons. It gives emphasis to what the letter has said about 'grace' (see the commentary on 1 Thess. 1.1). It ends with a reference only to the Lord Jesus Christ and omits any mention of God the Father; it is a form of blessing; it repeats the 'grace' of 1 Thess. 5.28 – with the addition of 'all'. It is an appropriate grace to conclude a letter which is one of affirmation against the background of the false alarm regarding the parousia. The Thessalonians have no need to fear the 'day of the Lord'. The prayer that Christ may be with them concerns every time and every situation, not least – at the end (see 1 Thess. 4.17; 5.10).

Postscript

This small commentary on the first extant Christian texts began with two aims: to try to understand the text in its original setting and to reflect on its significance for Christian living in the twenty-first century. My understanding of that remit is to encourage others to undertake the same journey of reflection and reaction. The remit does not actually require of me to answer all the questions, but only to assist the beginning of the process of responding to them. That does not mean that I have not personally made any discoveries in this short pilgrimage; indeed this postscript is a brief résumé of my own personal response.

Paul's recognition of the value of Christian community, both in practice and in theology, has found distinguished exponents in the last century. Its significance in providing companionship during periods of stress and change has been a classic feature of its pastoral function. Although we have had to understand the epistolary character of the thanksgivings and the prayer-wishes, the primary experiences which stand behind the epistolary forms represent one of the formative features of community Christian life and thought (Williams, pp. 239–64). It is as impossible to detach Paul's thanksgivings from their living roots as it is to detach Dietrich Bonhoeffer's spirituality from his *Letters and Papers from Prison*. And it is as impossible to detach Paul's worship, pastoral work and theology from his practical agenda as it is to detach Bonhoeffer's pattern of Christian life and community living from his *Act and Being* and his *Ethics* (Ford [Barton]). These influences and counter-balances are powerful memories from a reading of the Thessalonian correspondence, and rank among the major insights in my own study of the letters.

I asked initially if the earliest extant Christian document could in any way address the four greatest issues of contemporary life, as far as Christians might register their importance and ranking. The levels of Paul's relevance vary across the four major issues, but there is something to say on each of them. I do think that humanity is here for many purposes, and that was Paul's conviction: humanity lives and works defined by the divine nature and purpose. On a planet and in a universe raising a fund of questions concerning what we are here for, to respond positively to reality with every resource we have is in the end to discover more of what we have been given than we have contributed. This is perhaps the first generation which finds itself able not merely to discuss but also to respond to the issues of our cosmic future. Our world view is totally different from Paul's, and there is no way in which our cosmic future and his can be compared. Nevertheless, existence in its total reality can still be sensed, as it was by Paul, as a glorious, given privilege.

I do think that the co-existence of different faiths and cultures has a positive and even inspiring function, and that each religion has its own critique of idolatry within itself and with respect to others. Paul seems to have left open, or felt he could not close, most of the questions about the future apart from those which concerned the followers of Christ, and those who deliberately opposed them. He was able to take up that position because his view of ' the end' held that it could be discontinuous with everything before it. Everything depended ultimately on what God would do, and that was consolation to the Thessalonian converts. It is part of our Christian faith, and in no way a denial of it, to recognize what is ultimate as God's responsibility. To work with that kind of 'eschatology' would take considerable heat out of the 'other religions' debate, and let in a good deal of light.

I do believe that experts in the study of world economies are beginning to ask the kind of agenda questions which Paul in his small world of thought and action risked raising with his nascent communities. The floundering of 'first best' theories of the world economies and the failure of competitive markets to deliver what they promise has opened a new era (Stiglitz). That it is the duty of all local and national political communities to recognize the ethical and practical failings in former policies, and the role of democratic institutions to repair the damage they caused, is a burden we bear for the poor of the world. It will take the courage Paul had when identifying himself with the poor and risking himself and his shaping of the communities by the agenda he chose and realized.

I do believe that business, social and family life depend on trust and trustworthiness, faith and faithfulness. Paul discoveed how difficult it is to establish trust in relations within the communities and the cities where he worked. The socio-historical studies of the Thessalonian correspondence have opened our eyes to the corporate elements in Paul's thinking, and stand as a challenge to review the individualism which infects much of our Christian thought and practice and our biblical study. Modern sociological studies have performed a similar function for us in our situation, so that we can note the ways in which a state of trust can develop or decay, and we can respond effectively (Sztompka, pp. 146–90). We have been able to recognize the different stages of trust in the relations of the 'missionaries' and their converts. There is also a built-in critique in Paul's letters of our own understanding of trust. We have noted ways in which Paul's corporate insights begin from a different starting point from contemporary social studies. Paul's letters ask some serious questions of our contemporary social analyses, and make us aware of how comfortably we have accommodated ourselves to contemporary assumptions. The more that media attention (O'Neill, p. 10) and simplistic headlines impede rather than assist decision-making the more difficult our development of trust becomes. Trustworthiness and faithfulness, however, as Paul recognized, are written into the structure of existence as fundamental bases, and Paul traced them to the nature of God (White, p. 151).

As for the chaos of which Iris Murdoch and Simone Weil have written and which we have witnessed in different parts of our world and in the confusing perceptions surrounding our understanding of one another, the more I study city life in different parts of the ancient Roman Empire in the time of Paul the more amazed I am that Paul could still, despite the chaos around him, believe in the significance of human relationships and kinship patterns – and I take courage from that.

Central to all our work has been the question of holiness, its meaning for Paul and its meaning for us. Indeed, Rowan Williams has commented that holiness is the victory of God's faithfulness in the midst of disorder and imperfections. We can say, in fact, that all the above issues are for Paul, as for us, part of what is involved in holiness. Paul, like Bonhoeffer, uses the word 'holiness', recognizing that it carries for each the weight of centuries of expectation, explorations, errors and uncertainties. It is said that Bonhoeffer managed to present 'a habitable form of holiness, in which, utterly involved with God and with the world, one can be freed from the concern "to make something of oneself"' (Ford, p. 379). It was

Bonhoeffer also who observed the importance of allowing Scripture to reshape for us what holiness means. All in all, we have seen that possibility in Paul's first extant letters to a Christian community, in an astonishing achievement of mind, heart, energy, love and faith – and hope, and memory. I commend the pilgrimage he began.

BIBLIOGRAPHY

Commentaries

Best, E., 1972, *A Commentary on the First and Second Epistles to the Thessalonians*, Black's New Testament Commentaries, London, Black.

Bruce, F.F., 1982, *1 and 2 Thessalonians*, Word Biblical Commentary, Dallas, TX; Word.

Dobschutz, Ernst von, 1909, *Die Thessalonicherbriefe*, Göttingen, Vandenhoeck & Ruprecht.

Frame, J.E., 1912, *The Epistles of St Paul to the Thessalonians*, ICC, Edinburgh, T&T Clark.

Haufe, G., 1999, *Der erste Brief des Paulus an die Thessalonicher*, Theologischer Handkommentar zum N.T., Leipzig, Evangelische Verlagsanstalt.

Holtz, T., 1986, *Der erste Brief an die Thessalonicher*, Evangelisch-katholiker Kommentar zum N.T., Zürich, Benziger.

Malherbe, A.J., 2000, *The Letters to the Thessalonians*, The Anchor Bible, New York, Doubleday.

Marshall, I.H. 1981, *1 & 2 Thessalonians*, New Century Bible, Grand Rapids, MI, Eerdmans.

Menken, M.J., 1994, *2 Thessalonians*, New Testament Readings, London, Routledge.

Wanamaker, C.A., 1990, *The Epistles to the Thessalonians. A Commentary on the Greek Text*, Grand Rapids, MI, Eerdmans.

Books and articles

Alexander, L., 2001, 'Acts', in *The Oxford Bible Commentary* (eds Barton, J. and Muddiman, J.), Oxford, Oxford University Press, pp. 1028–61.

Ascough, R.C., 2003, *Paul's Macedonian Associations. The Social Context of Philippians and 1 Thessalonians*, Tübingen, Mohr Siebeck.

——2005, 'A Question of Death: Paul's Community-Building Language in 1 Thessalonians 4.13–18', *Novum Testamentum* 47, pp. 509–30.

Aus, R.J., 1973, 'The Liturgical Background of the Necessity and Propriety of Giving Thanks According to 2 Thess. 1.3', *Journal of Biblical Literature* 92, pp. 432–38.

——1976, 'The Relevance of Isaiah 66:7 to Revelation 12 and 2 Thessalonians 1', *Zeitschrift für die neutestamentliche Wissenschaft*, 67, pp. 252–68.

Barclay, J.M., 1993, 'Conflict in Thessalonica', *Catholic Biblical Quarterly* 55, pp. 512–30.

——1992, 'Thessalonica and Corinth: Social Contrasts in Pauline Christianity', *Journal for the Study of the New Testament* 47, pp. 49–74.

——2003, 'That you may not grieve, as do the rest, who have no hope (1 Thess. 4.13): Death and Early Christian Identity', in *Not in the Word Alone. The First Epistle to the Thessalonians* (ed. Hooker-Stacey, M.), Monograph Series, Rome, 'Benedictina' Publishing, pp. 155–66.

Barrett, C.K., 1994–1999, *Acts. International Commentary* (2 vols), Edinburgh, T&T Clark.

Barton, S.C. (ed.), 2003, *Holiness, Past and Present*, Edinburgh, T&T Clark International.

——'Dislocating and Relocating Holiness: A New Testament Study', in *Holiness, Past and Present* (ed. Barton, S.C.), Edinburgh; T&T Clark International, pp. 193–213.

Bassler, J.M., 1984 'The Enigmatic Sign: 2 Thessalonians 1:5', *Catholic Biblical Quarterly* 46, pp. 496–510.

Berger, U., 2004, 'Der Zorn Gottes in der Prophetie und Poesie Israels auf dem Hintergrund altorientalischer Vorstellungen', *Biblica* 85, pp. 305–30.

Blumenthal, C., 2005, 'Was sagt 1 Thess 1.9b–10 über die Adressaten des 1 Thess? Literarische und historische Erwägungen', *New Testament Studies* 51, pp. 96–105.

Bockmuehl, M., 2003, '1 Thess. 2.14–16 and the Church in Jerusalem', in *Not in the Word Alone. The First Epistle to the Thessalonians* (ed. Hooker-Stacey, M.), Monograph Series, Rome, 'Benedictina' Publishing, pp. 55–88.

Breytenbach, C., 2003, 'Der Danksagungsbericht des Paulus über den Gottesglauben der Thessalonicher: 1 Thess. 1.2–10', in *Not in the Word Alone. The First Epistle to the Thessalonians* (ed. Hooker-

Stacey, M.), Monograph Series, Rome, 'Benedictina' Publishing, pp. 3–24.

Burke, T.J., 2003, *Family Matters. A Socio-Historical Study of Kinship Metaphors in I Thessalonians*, London, T&T Clark International.

Collins, R.F., 1990 *The Thessalonian Correspondence*, Bibliotheca ephemeridum theologicarum lovaniensium, Leuven, Leuven University Press.

Conradi, P.J., 1989, *The Saint and the Artist*, London, HarperCollins.

Crowder, C., 2003, ' "Idea of the Holy" Revisited', in *Holiness, Past and Present* (ed. Barton, S.C.), Edinburgh, T&T Clark International, pp. 22–47.

Donfried, K.P., 1985, 'The Cults of Thessalonica and the Thessalonian Correspondence', *New Testament Studies* 31, pp. 316–56.

——2000, (edited with Beutler, J.), *The Thessalonians Debate. Methodological Discord or Methodological Synthesis?*, Grand Rapids, MI, Eerdmans.

——2002, *Paul, Thessalonica, and Early Christianity*, London, T&T Clark (Continuum Imprint).

Dunn, J.D.G., 1988, *The Epistle to the Romans 1–8 and 9–16*, Word Bible Commentary, Dallas, TX, Word.

Ellingworth, P. and Nida, E., 1975, *A Translator's Handbook on Paul's Letters to the Thessalonians*, Stuttgart, United Bible Society.

Esler, P.F., 2001, '1 and 2 Thessalonians', in *The Oxford Bible Commentary* (eds Barton J. and Muddiman, J.), Oxford, Oxford University Press, pp. 1199–220.

Fee, G.E., 1991, *'On Text and Commentary on 1 and 2 Thessalonians'*, SBL Seminar Papers 31, Atlanta, GA, Scholars Press.

Ford D., 2003, 'Bonhoeffer, Holiness and Politics', in *Holiness, Past and Present* (ed. Barton, S.C.), Edinburgh, T&T Clark International, pp. 363–82.

Giblin, N., 1967, *The Threat to Faith: An Exegetical and Theological Re-Examination of 2 Thessalonians*, Rome, Pontifical Biblical Institute.

Harrison, J.R., 2003, *Paul's Language of Grace in its Graeco-Roman Context*, Tübingen, Mohr Siebeck.

Heidegger, M., 1960, 'Phänomenologische Explikation des ersten Briefes an die Thessaloniker' (lectures during 1920–21), in *Phänomenologie des Religiosen Lebens*, Frankfurt, Klostermann Gesamtausgabe Band 60, pp. 91–150.

Holmes, J. G. and Ellard, J. H., 1985, 'Boundary Roles and Intergroup Conflict', in *Psychology of Intergroup Relations* (ed. Worchel, S.), Illinois, Nelson-Hall.

Hooker-Stacey M.D. (ed.), 2003, *Not in the Word Alone. The First Epistle to the Thessalonians*, Monograph Series, Rome, 'Benedictina' Publishing.

Hoppe, R., 2004, 'Der Topos der Prophetenverfolgung bei Paulus', *New Testament Studies* 50, pp. 535–49.

Horbury, W., 1982, 'I Thessalonians ii.3 as Rebutting the Charge of False Prophecy', *Journal of Theological Studies* 33, pp. 492–508.

Horrell, D.G., 1996, *The Social Ethos of the Corinthian Correspondence: Interests and Ideology from 1 Corinthians to 1 Clement*, Edinburgh, T&T Clark.

——2004, 'Domestic Space and Christian Meetings at Corinth. Imagining New Contexts and the Buildings East of the Theatre', *New Testament Studies* 50, pp. 349–69.

Hughes, F.W., 1989, *Early Christian Rhetoric and 2 Thessalonians*, Journal for the Study of the New Testament Supplement 30, Sheffield, JSOT Press.

Isaacs, M., 1976, *The Concept of Spirit*, London, Heythrop College Publishing.

Jewett, R., 1986, *The Thessalonian Correspondence. Pauline Rhetoric and Millenarian Piety*, Philadelphia, Fortress Press.

Kim, S., 2001, 'The Jesus Tradition in 1 Thess 4:1–5:11', A Paper to the Seminar on The Thessalonian Correspondence, SNTS, Montreal.

Lambrecht, J., 2000, 'Thanksgivings in 1 Thessalonians 1–3', in *The Thessalonians Debate. Methodological Discord or Methodological Synthesis?* (eds Donfried, K.P. and Beutler, J.), Grand Rapids, MI, Eerdmans, pp. 135–62.

Lieu, J.M., 1994, 'Do God-fearers make good Christians?' in *Crossing the Boundaries*, Essays in Honour of Michael Goulder (eds Porter, S.E., Joye, P., and Orton, D.), Leiden, Brill, pp. 329–45.

——1996, *Image and Reality. The Jews in the World of the Christians of the Second Century*, Edinburgh, T&T Clark.

Long, F.J., 2004, *Ancient Rhetoric and Paul's Apology*, Society of New Testament Studies Monograph Series 131, Cambridge, Cambridge University Press.

Malherbe, A.J., 1986, *Moral Exhortation. A Greco-Roman Source Book*. Philadelphia, Westminster Press.

Marguerat, D., 2003, 'Imiter l'apôtre, mère et père de la communauté: 1 Thess 2:1–12', in *Not in the Word Alone. The First Epistle to the Thessalonians* (ed. Hooker-Stacey, M.), Monograph Series, Rome, 'Benedictina' Publishing, pp. 25–54.

Marshall, I.H., 1990, 'Election and Calling to Salvation in 1 and 2 Thessalonians', in *The Thessalonian Correspondence*, Bibliotheca ephemeridum theologicarum lovaniensium (ed. Collins, R.F.), Leuven, Leuven University Press, pp. 259–76.

Meggitt, J.J., 1998, *Paul, Poverty and Survival*, Edinburgh, T&T Clark.

Mitchell, M., 2000, 'The Thessalonian Letters', in *The Cambridge Handbook on Paul* (ed. Dunn, J.D.G.), Cambridge, Cambridge University Press.

Moule, C.F.D., 1953, *An Idiom-Book of New Testament Greek*, Cambridge, Cambridge University Press.

Murphy-O'Connor, J., 1996, *Paul: A Critical Life*, Oxford, Clarendon Press.

Nicholl, C.R., 2004, *From Hope to Despair in Thessalonica*, Society of New Testament Studies Monograph Series 126, Cambridge, Cambridge University Press.

O'Brien, P., 1977, *Introductory Thanksgivings in the Letters of Paul*, Novum Testamentum Supplement 49, Leiden, Brill.

O'Neill, O., 2002, *A Question of Trust*, Cambridge, Cambridge University Press.

Oestreich, B., 2004 'Leseanweisungen in Briefen als Mittel des Gestaltung von Beziehungen (1 Thess 5:27)', *New Testament Studies* 50, pp. 224–45.

Plevnik, J., 1979, 'I Thess 5:1–11: Its Authenticity, Intention and Message', *Biblica* 60, pp. 71–90.

Porter, S.E., 1997, *Handbook of Classical Rhetoric in the Hellenistic Period 330 B.C.–A.D. 400*, Leiden, Brill.

Powys, D.J., 2002, *'Hell': A Hard Look at a Hard Question. The Fate of the Unrighteous in New Testament Thought*, London, Paternoster Press.

Richardson, N., 1994, *Paul's Language about God*, Journal for the Study of the New Testament Supplement Series 99, Sheffield, Sheffield Academic Press.

Riesner, R., 1994, *Paul's Early Period. Chronology, Mission Strategy, Theology* (trans. Stott, D.), Grand Rapids, MI: Eerdmans.

Selwyn, E.G., 1958, *The First Epistle of Peter*, London, Macmillan.

Söding, T., 1992, *Die Trias: Glaube, Hoffnung, Liebe bei Paulus. Eine exegetische Studie*, Stuttgart: Verlag katholisches Bibelwerk.

Standaert, B., 2003, 'La prima lettera ai Tessalonicesi – sorgente di vita spirituale', in *Not in the Word Alone. The First Espistle to the Thessalonians* (ed. Hooker-Stacey, M.), Monograph Series, Rome, 'Benedictina' Publishing, pp. 167–83.

Stiglitz, J.E., 2004, 'Ethics and the Economics of Globalisation', Tanner Lecture on Human Values, Oxford.

Still, T.D., 1999, *Conflict at Thessalonika. A Pauline Church and its Neighbourhood*, Journal for the Study of the New Testament Supplement Series 183, Sheffield, JSOT Press.

Sztompka, P., 1999, *Trust. A Sociological Study.* Cambridge, Cambridge University Press.

Theissen, G., 1982, *The Social Setting of Pauline Christianity* (ed. and trans. Schütz, J.), Edinburgh, T&T Clark.

Thiselton, A.C., 2000, *The First Epistle to the Corinthians*, The New International Greek Testament Commentary, Grand Rapids, MI: Eerdmans.

Tomson, P. J., 2003, 'Paul's Practical Instruction in 1 Thess 4:1–12 read in a Hellenistic and Jewish perspective', in *Not in the Word Alone. The First Epistle to the Thessalonians* (ed. Hooker-Stacey, M.), Monograph Series, Rome, 'Benedictina' Publishing, pp. 89–130.

Triandis, H. C., 1985, 'Are there important omissions?', in *Psychology of Intergroup Relations* (ed. Worchel, S.), Illinois, Nelson-Hall, pp. 373–8.

Wainwright, G., 2003, *Eucharist and Eschatology*, Peterborough, Epworth Press.

Wedderburn, A.J.M., 1987, *Baptism and Resurrection*, Tübingen, Mohr Siebeck.

——2002, 'Paul's Collection: Chronology and History', *New Testament Studies* 48, pp. 95–110.

White, V., 2002, *Identity*, London, SCM Press.

Williams, R., 2000, 'Interiority and Epiphany: A Reading in New Testament Ethics', in *On Christian Theology.* Oxford, Blackwell. pp. 239–64.

Wischmeyer, O., 2004, *Von Ben Sira zu Paulus*, Tübingen, Mohr Siebeck.

Wold, B.G., 2004, 'Reconsidering an Aspect of the Title Kyrios in the Light of Sapiential Fragment 4Q416 2iii', *Zeitschrift für die neutestamentliche Wissenschaft* 34, pp. 149–60.

Worchel, S., 1985, *Psychology of Intergroup Relations*, Illinois, Nelson-Hall.

——1985, 'The Role of Cooperation in Reducing Intergroup Conflict', in *Psychology of Intergroup Relations* (ed. Worchel, S.), Illinois, Nelson-Hall, pp. 283–304.